Calculus II Workbook
100 Problems with full solutions

covering

Volume
Integration Techniques
Integration Applications
Introductory Differential Equations
Sequences and Series

N. Rimmer

Cover Design: Rob King
Interior Layout: Tony Bradford
ISBN 978-1-938950-55-1

Greater Is He Publishing
9824 E. Washington St.
Chagrin Falls, Ohio 44023
Phone: 216.288.9315
www.GreaterIsHePublishing.com

CONTENTS

PREFACE

This is a collection of my Calculus II midterm exam problems. The solutions are written by me using methods taught during lecture. For further explanation as to the why behind the methods, please see CalcCoach.com. There you will find my lecture notes, lecture videos, and premium problem solution videos explaining in detail the thought process involved in solving 100 different problems. If your goal is to gain a good understanding of the topics typically found in a Calculus II class, then the combination of this workbook and the other three components found on CalcCoach.com should help tremendously. If you have any thoughts or concerns, don't hesitate to contact me.

Nakia Rimmer

SECTION I

Volume

Arc Length

Surface Area of Revolution

Center of Mass

Integration by Parts

1.1. Find the volume of the solid that lies between planes perpendicular to the x – axis at $x = 0$ and $x = 1$. The cross sections of the solid perpendicular to the x – axis between these planes are semicircles whose diameters run from the curve $y = x^3$ to the curve $y = x$.

(A) $\dfrac{\pi}{16}$ (C) $\dfrac{\pi}{60}$ (E) $\dfrac{\pi}{40}$ (G) $\dfrac{\pi}{105}$

(B) $\dfrac{\pi}{80}$ (D) $\dfrac{\pi}{24}$ (F) $\dfrac{\pi}{240}$ (H) $\dfrac{\pi}{120}$

1.1. Find the volume of the solid that lies between planes perpendicular to the x – axis at $x = 0$ and $x = 1$. The cross sections of the solid perpendicular to the x – axis between these planes are semicircles whose diameters run from the curve $y = x^3$ to the curve $y = x$.

(A) $\dfrac{\pi}{16}$

(C) $\dfrac{\pi}{60}$

(E) $\dfrac{\pi}{40}$

(G) $\dfrac{\pi}{105}$

(B) $\dfrac{\pi}{80}$

(D) $\dfrac{\pi}{24}$

(F) $\dfrac{\pi}{240}$

(H) $\dfrac{\pi}{120}$

The diameter d is the distance between the curves
$$d = x - x^3$$

The radius r is half of the distance between the curves
$$r \approx \frac{x - x^3}{2}$$

The shape is a semicircle so the area A is
$$A(r) = \frac{1}{2}\pi r^2$$
$$A(x) = \frac{\pi}{2}\left(\frac{x - x^3}{2}\right)^2$$
$$A(x) = \frac{\pi}{2}\cdot\frac{1}{4}\left(x - x^3\right)^2$$
$$A(x) = \frac{\pi}{8}\left(x - x^3\right)\left(x - x^3\right)$$

$$\boxed{A(x) = \frac{\pi}{8}\left(x^2 - 2x^4 + x^6\right)}$$

$$V = \int_a^b A(x)\,dx$$
cross-sectional area formula

$$V = \int_0^1 \frac{\pi}{8}\left(x^2 - 2x^4 + x^6\right)dx$$

$$V = \frac{\pi}{8}\left[\frac{x^3}{3} - \frac{2x^5}{5} + \frac{x^7}{7}\right]_0^1$$

$$V = \frac{\pi}{8}\left[\frac{1}{3} - \frac{2}{5} + \frac{1}{7}\right] = \frac{\pi}{8}\left[\frac{1\cdot35}{3\cdot35} - \frac{2\cdot21}{5\cdot21} + \frac{1\cdot15}{7\cdot15}\right]$$

$$V = \frac{\pi}{8}\left[\frac{35 - 42 + 15}{105}\right] = \frac{\pi}{8}\left[\frac{50 - 42}{105}\right] = \frac{\pi}{8}\left[\frac{8}{105}\right]$$

$$\boxed{V = \frac{\pi}{105}\ \text{units}^3}$$

1.2. Find the volume of the solid generated by revolving the region in the first quadrant bounded by $y = x^2 + 1, x = 0,$ and $y = 2$ about the line $y = 2$

(A) $\dfrac{4\pi}{5}$

(C) $\dfrac{8\pi}{15}$

(E) $\dfrac{12\pi}{5}$

(G) $\dfrac{4\pi}{15}$

(B) $\dfrac{7\pi}{10}$

(D) $\dfrac{2\pi}{3}$

(F) $\dfrac{2\pi}{15}$

(H) $\dfrac{2\pi}{5}$

1.2. Find the volume of the solid generated by revolving the region in the first quadrant bounded by $y = x^2 + 1, x = 0,$ and $y = 2$ about the line $y = 2$

(A) $\dfrac{4\pi}{5}$ (C) $\dfrac{8\pi}{15}$ (E) $\dfrac{12\pi}{5}$ (G) $\dfrac{4\pi}{15}$

(B) $\dfrac{7\pi}{10}$ (D) $\dfrac{2\pi}{3}$ (F) $\dfrac{2\pi}{15}$ (H) $\dfrac{2\pi}{5}$

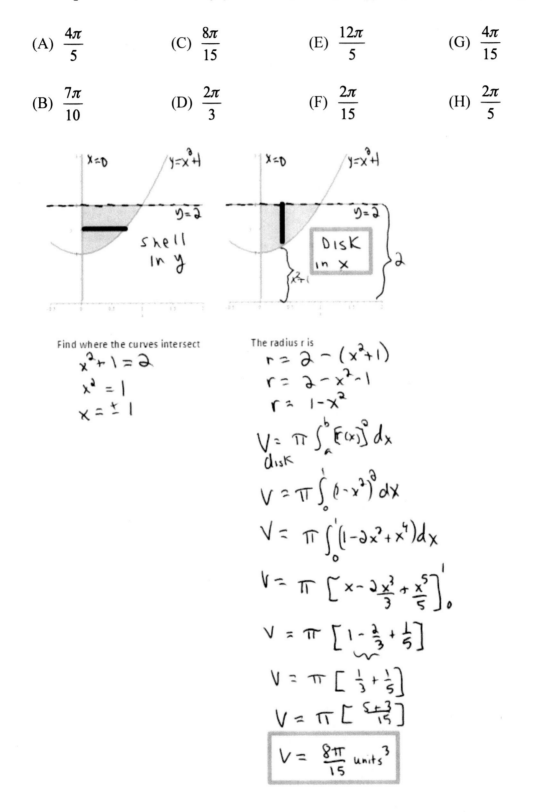

Find where the curves intersect

$$x^2 + 1 = 2$$
$$x^2 = 1$$
$$x = \pm 1$$

The radius r is

$$r = 2 - (x^2 + 1)$$
$$r = 2 - x^2 - 1$$
$$r = 1 - x^2$$

$$V = \pi \int_a^b [F(x)]^2 \, dx$$
disk

$$V = \pi \int_0^1 (1 - x^2)^2 \, dx$$

$$V = \pi \int_0^1 (1 - 2x^2 + x^4) \, dx$$

$$V = \pi \left[x - \frac{2x^3}{3} + \frac{x^5}{5} \right]_0^1$$

$$V = \pi \left[1 - \frac{2}{3} + \frac{1}{5} \right]$$

$$V = \pi \left[\frac{1}{3} + \frac{1}{5} \right]$$

$$V = \pi \left[\frac{5 + 3}{15} \right]$$

$$\boxed{V = \frac{8\pi}{15} \text{ units}^3}$$

8

1.3. Find the volume of the solid generated when the region bounded by $y = x^2 + 1$, $y = -x + 1$ and $x = 1$ is revolved about the y – axis.

(A) 1

(B) π

(C) $\dfrac{\pi}{2}$

(D) $\dfrac{\pi}{6}$

(E) $\dfrac{7\pi}{6}$

(F) $\dfrac{\pi}{4}$

(G) $\dfrac{\pi}{8}$

(H) $\dfrac{5\pi}{6}$

1.3. Find the volume of the solid generated when the region bounded by $y = x^2 + 1$, $y = -x + 1$ and $x = 1$ is revolved about the y – axis.

(A) 1

(C) $\dfrac{\pi}{2}$

(E) $\dfrac{7\pi}{6}$

(G) $\dfrac{\pi}{8}$

(B) π

(D) $\dfrac{\pi}{6}$

(F) $\dfrac{\pi}{4}$

(H) $\dfrac{5\pi}{6}$

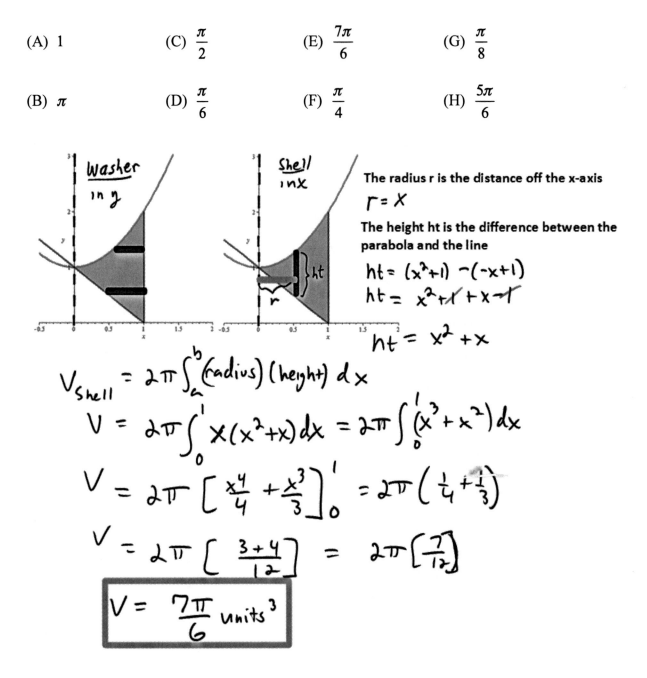

The radius r is the distance off the x-axis

$r = X$

The height ht is the difference between the parabola and the line

$ht = (x^2+1) - (-x+1)$

$ht = x^2 + \cancel{1} + x - \cancel{1}$

$ht = x^2 + x$

$V_{Shell} = 2\pi \int_a^b (radius)(height)\, dx$

$V = 2\pi \int_0^1 x(x^2+x)\, dx = 2\pi \int_0^1 (x^3 + x^2)\, dx$

$V = 2\pi \left[\dfrac{x^4}{4} + \dfrac{x^3}{3} \right]_0^1 = 2\pi \left(\dfrac{1}{4} + \dfrac{1}{3} \right)$

$V = 2\pi \left[\dfrac{3+4}{12} \right] = 2\pi \left[\dfrac{7}{12} \right]$

$\boxed{V = \dfrac{7\pi}{6} \text{ units}^3}$

1.4. Find the volume of the solid generated by revolving the region bounded by $y = 2 + \sqrt{x-1}, x = 2, x = 5,$ and $y = 2,$ about the x – axis.

(A) $\dfrac{17\pi}{6}$

(B) 24π

(C) $\dfrac{11\pi}{2}$

(D) $\dfrac{145\pi}{6}$

(E) $\dfrac{15\pi}{2}$

(F) $\dfrac{151\pi}{6}$

(G) 40π

(H) $\dfrac{157\pi}{6}$

1.4. Find the volume of the solid generated by revolving the region bounded by $y = 2 + \sqrt{x-1}, x = 2, y = 5,$ and $y = 2,$ about the x – axis.

(A) $\dfrac{17\pi}{6}$ (C) $\dfrac{11\pi}{2}$ (E) $\dfrac{15\pi}{2}$ (G) 40π

(B) 24π (D) $\dfrac{145\pi}{6}$ (F) $\dfrac{151\pi}{6}$ (H) $\dfrac{157\pi}{6}$

Shell
in y

washer
in x

$y = 2 + \sqrt{x-1}$

Take $y = \sqrt{x}$
shift up 2
$2 + \sqrt{x-1}$ shift right 1

Outer radius
$R(x) = 2 + \sqrt{x-1}$

Inner radius
$r(x) = 2$

$V_{washer} = \pi \int_a^b \left[(R(x))^2 - (r(x))^2 \right] dx$

$V = \pi \int_2^5 \left((2+\sqrt{x-1})^2 - 2^2 \right) dx$

$V = \pi \int_2^5 \left(4 + 4\sqrt{x-1} + (x-1) - 4 \right) dx$

$V = \pi \int_2^5 \left(x - 1 + 4\sqrt{x-1} \right) dx$

$V = \pi \left[\dfrac{x^2}{2} - x + \dfrac{4 \cdot 2}{3}(x-1)^{3/2} \right]_2^5$

$4^{3/2} = (4^{1/2})^3$
$= 2^3 = 8$

$V = \pi \left[\left(\dfrac{25}{2} - 5 + \dfrac{8}{3}(4)^{3/2} \right) - \left(2 - 2 + \dfrac{8}{3} \right) \right]$

$V = \pi \left[\dfrac{25}{2} - 5 + \dfrac{64}{3} - \dfrac{8}{3} \right]$

$V = \pi \left[\dfrac{25}{2} - 5 + \dfrac{56}{3} \right] = \pi \left[\dfrac{75 - 30 + 112}{6} \right]$

$\boxed{V = \dfrac{157\pi}{6} \text{ units}^3}$

12

1.5. Find the volume of the solid generated by revolving the region bounded by $y = 4 - x^2$, $y = 4$, and $x = 2$, about the x – axis.

(A) $\dfrac{74\pi}{5}$ (C) $\dfrac{97\pi}{12}$ (E) $\dfrac{124\pi}{15}$ (G) $\dfrac{224\pi}{15}$

(B) $\dfrac{115\pi}{9}$ (D) $\dfrac{85\pi}{6}$ (F) $\dfrac{109\pi}{9}$ (H) $\dfrac{152\pi}{5}$

1.5. Find the volume of the solid generated by revolving the region bounded by $y = 4 - x^2$, $y = 4$, and $x = 2$, about the x – axis.

(A) $\dfrac{74\pi}{5}$

(C) $\dfrac{97\pi}{12}$

(E) $\dfrac{124\pi}{15}$

(G) $\dfrac{224\pi}{15}$

(B) $\dfrac{115\pi}{9}$

(D) $\dfrac{85\pi}{6}$

(F) $\dfrac{109\pi}{9}$

(H) $\dfrac{152\pi}{5}$

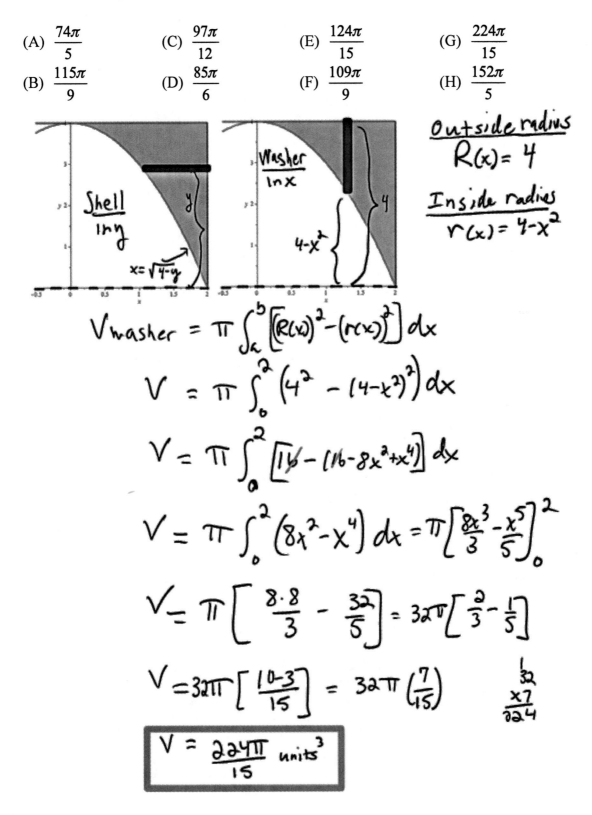

Outside radius
$R(x) = 4$

Inside radius
$r(x) = 4 - x^2$

Shell in y

$x = \sqrt{4-y}$

Washer in x

$4 - x^2$

$$V_{washer} = \pi \int_a^b \left[(R(x))^2 - (r(x))^2 \right] dx$$

$$V = \pi \int_0^2 \left(4^2 - (4-x^2)^2 \right) dx$$

$$V = \pi \int_0^2 \left[16 - (16 - 8x^2 + x^4) \right] dx$$

$$V = \pi \int_0^2 \left(8x^2 - x^4 \right) dx = \pi \left[\frac{8x^3}{3} - \frac{x^5}{5} \right]_0^2$$

$$V = \pi \left[\frac{8 \cdot 8}{3} - \frac{32}{5} \right] = 32\pi \left[\frac{2}{3} - \frac{1}{5} \right]$$

$$V = 32\pi \left[\frac{10-3}{15} \right] = 32\pi \left(\frac{7}{15} \right) \qquad \begin{array}{r} 32 \\ \times 7 \\ \hline 224 \end{array}$$

$$\boxed{V = \frac{224\pi}{15} \text{ units}^3}$$

1.6. Find the volume of the solid generated by revolving the region bounded by $y = \ln x$, $y = 0$, and $x = e$ about the x-axis.

(A) $\dfrac{\pi}{2}(e+1)$ (C) $\pi(4-e)$ (E) $\dfrac{\pi}{4}e+2\pi$ (G) π

(B) 2π (D) $\dfrac{\pi}{2}e$ (F) $\pi(e-2)$ (H) πe

1.6. Find the volume of the solid generated by revolving the region bounded by $y = \ln x$, $y = 0$, and $x = e$ about the x – axis.

(A) $\dfrac{\pi}{2}(e+1)$ (C) $\pi(4-e)$ (E) $\dfrac{\pi}{4}e + 2\pi$ (G) π

(B) 2π (D) $\dfrac{\pi}{2}e$ (F) $\pi(e-2)$ (H) πe

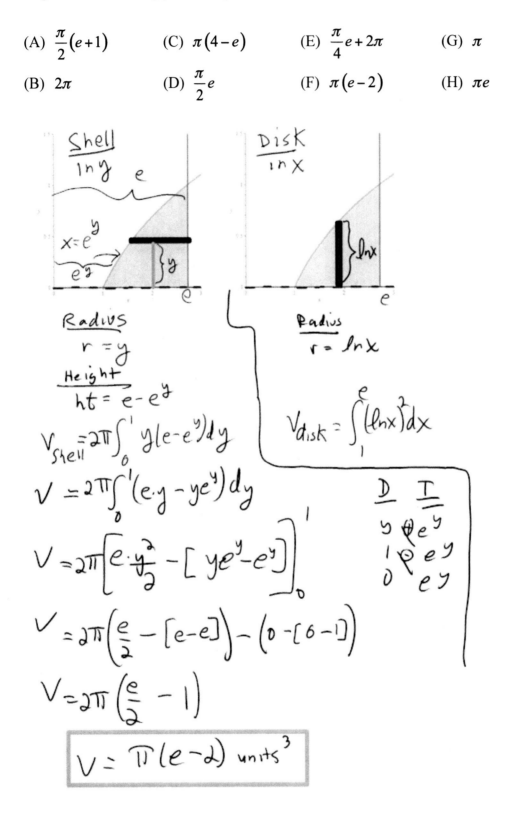

Shell
$\ln y$

Disk
$\ln x$

Radius
$r = y$

Height
$ht = e - e^y$

$V_{Shell} = 2\pi \int_0^1 y(e - e^y)\,dy$

$V = 2\pi \int_0^1 (e \cdot y - y e^y)\,dy$

$V = 2\pi \left[e \cdot \dfrac{y^2}{2} - [y e^y - e^y] \right]_0^1$

$V = 2\pi \left(\dfrac{e}{2} - [e-e] \right) - \left(0 - [6-1] \right)$

$V = 2\pi \left(\dfrac{e}{2} - 1 \right)$

$\boxed{V = \pi(e-2) \text{ units}^3}$

Radius
$r = \ln x$

$V_{disk} = \int_1^e (\ln x)^2\,dx$

$\dfrac{D}{} \quad \dfrac{I}{}$

$y \quad \oplus e^y$

$1 \quad \ominus e^y$

$0 \quad e^y$

16

1.7. **Setup but DON'T solve.** Find the volume of the solid generated by revolving the region bounded by $y = \sqrt{x+3}, y = 0,$ and $x + y = 3,$ about the line $y = -2$. **Setup but DON'T solve.**

1.7. **Setup but DON'T solve.** Find the volume of the solid generated by revolving the region bounded by $y = \sqrt{x+3}$, $y = 0$, and $x + y = 3$, about the line $y = -2$. **Setup but DON'T solve.**

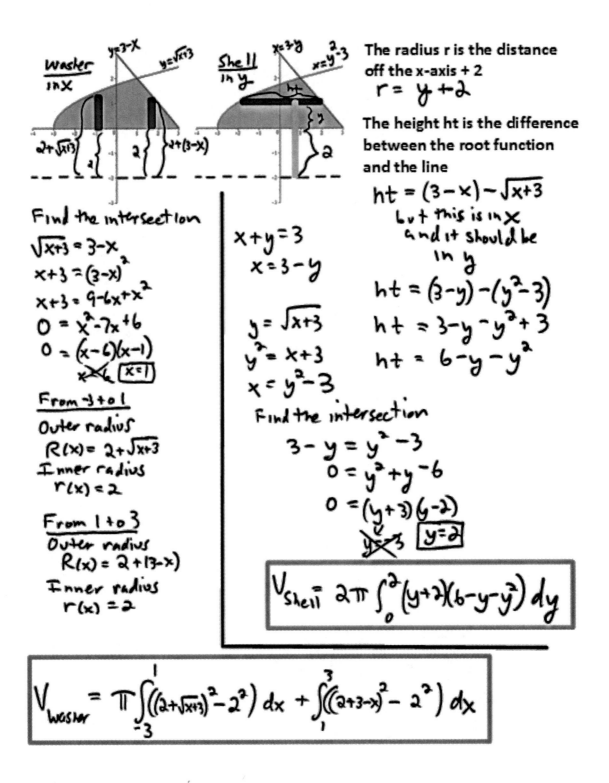

Washer
in X

Find the intersection
$\sqrt{x+3} = 3-x$
$x+3 = (3-x)^2$
$x+3 = 9-6x+x^2$
$0 = x^2 - 7x + 6$
$0 = (x-6)(x-1)$
$x=6$ $\boxed{x=1}$

From -3 to 1
Outer radius
$R(x) = 2 + \sqrt{x+3}$
Inner radius
$r(x) = 2$

From 1 to 3
Outer radius
$R(x) = 2 + (3-x)$
Inner radius
$r(x) = 2$

Shell
in y

$x + y = 3$
$x = 3 - y$

$y = \sqrt{x+3}$
$y^2 = x+3$
$x = y^2 - 3$

Find the intersection
$3 - y = y^2 - 3$
$0 = y^2 + y - 6$
$0 = (y+3)(y-2)$
$y=-3$ $\boxed{y=2}$

The radius r is the distance off the x-axis + 2
$r = y + 2$

The height ht is the difference between the root function and the line
$ht = (3-x) - \sqrt{x+3}$
but this is in X and it should be in y
$ht = (3-y) - (y^2 - 3)$
$ht = 3 - y - y^2 + 3$
$ht = 6 - y - y^2$

$$V_{shell} = 2\pi \int_0^2 (y+2)(6-y-y^2)\, dy$$

$$V_{washer} = \pi \int_{-3}^{1} \left((2+\sqrt{x+3})^2 - 2^2 \right) dx + \int_1^3 \left((2+3-x)^2 - 2^2 \right) dx$$

18

1.8. The base of a solid is in the first quadrant between the curve $y = x^2$ and the curve $y = \sqrt{x}$ for $0 \leq x \leq 1$. The cross sections of the solid perpendicular to the x – axis are isosceles right triangles whose leg runs between the curves. Find the volume of the solid.

(A) $\dfrac{3}{70}$ (C) $\dfrac{\sqrt{2}}{25}$ (E) $\dfrac{9}{35}$ (G) $\dfrac{37}{70}$

(B) $\dfrac{3}{35}$ (D) $\dfrac{9}{140}$ (F) $\dfrac{9}{70}$ (H) $\dfrac{9\sqrt{3}}{280}$

1.8. The base of a solid is in the first quadrant between the curve $y = x^2$ and the curve $y = \sqrt{x}$ for $0 \le x \le 1$. The cross sections of the solid perpendicular to the x – axis are isosceles right triangles whose leg runs between the curves. Find the volume of the solid.

(A) $\dfrac{3}{70}$ (C) $\dfrac{\sqrt{2}}{25}$ (E) $\dfrac{9}{35}$ (G) $\dfrac{37}{70}$

(B) $\dfrac{3}{35}$ (D) $\dfrac{9}{140}$ (F) $\dfrac{9}{70}$ (H) $\dfrac{9\sqrt{3}}{280}$

The leg length s is the difference between the root function and the parabola

$S = \sqrt{x} - x^2$

$A(s) = \frac{1}{2} \cdot s \cdot s$

$A(s) = \frac{1}{2} s^2$

$A(x) = \frac{1}{2} \left(\sqrt{x} - x^2 \right)^2$

$A(x) = \frac{1}{2} \left(x - 2\sqrt{x} \cdot x^2 + x^4 \right)$

$A(x) = \frac{1}{2} \left(x - 2 x^{5/2} + x^4 \right)$

$V = \int_a^b A(x)\, dx = \int_0^1 \frac{1}{2} \left(x - 2x^{5/2} + x^4 \right) dx$

$V = \frac{1}{2} \left[\frac{x^2}{2} - 2 \cdot \frac{2}{7} x^{7/2} + \frac{x^5}{5} \right]_0^1$

$V = \frac{1}{2} \left[\left(\frac{1}{2} - \frac{4}{7} + \frac{1}{5} \right) - 0 \right]$

$V = \frac{1}{2} \left[\frac{35 - 40 + 14}{70} \right]$

$\boxed{V = \dfrac{9}{140} \ \text{units}^3}$

1.9. Find the volume of the solid generated by revolving the region bounded by $y = x$, $y = -x$, and $x = 2$, about the line $x = -3$.

(A) $\dfrac{74\pi}{4}$ (C) $\dfrac{97\pi}{12}$ (E) $\dfrac{26\pi}{3}$ (G) $\dfrac{208\pi}{3}$

(B) $\dfrac{115\pi}{3}$ (D) $\dfrac{85\pi}{6}$ (F) $\dfrac{104\pi}{3}$ (H) $\dfrac{52\pi}{9}$

1.9. Find the volume of the solid generated by revolving the region bounded by $y = x$, $y = -x$, and $x = 2$, about the line $x = -3$.

(A) $\dfrac{74\pi}{4}$ (C) $\dfrac{97\pi}{12}$ (E) $\dfrac{26\pi}{3}$ (G) $\dfrac{208\pi}{3}$

(B) $\dfrac{115\pi}{3}$ (D) $\dfrac{85\pi}{6}$ (F) $\dfrac{104\pi}{3}$ (H) $\dfrac{52\pi}{9}$

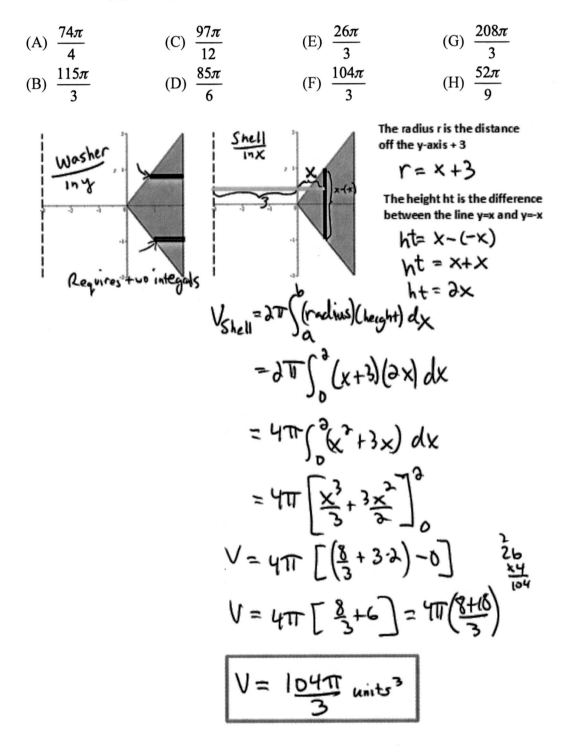

Washer
in y

Requires two integrals

Shell
in x

The radius r is the distance off the y-axis + 3

$r = x + 3$

The height ht is the difference between the line y=x and y=-x

$ht = x - (-x)$
$ht = x + x$
$ht = 2x$

$$V_{Shell} = 2\pi \int_a^b (\text{radius})(\text{height})\, dx$$

$$= 2\pi \int_0^2 (x+3)(2x)\, dx$$

$$= 4\pi \int_0^2 (x^2 + 3x)\, dx$$

$$= 4\pi \left[\frac{x^3}{3} + \frac{3x^2}{2} \right]_0^2$$

$$V = 4\pi \left[\left(\frac{8}{3} + 3\cdot 2 \right) - 0 \right]$$

$$V = 4\pi \left[\frac{8}{3} + 6 \right] = 4\pi \left(\frac{8+18}{3} \right)$$

$$\boxed{V = \frac{104\pi}{3}\ units^3}$$

$\begin{matrix} 26 \\ \times 4 \\ \hline 104 \end{matrix}$

1.10. Find the volume of the solid generated by revolving the region bounded by $y = \sqrt{x}$, $x = 0$, and $y = 1$ about the line $y = -1$.

(A) $\dfrac{7\pi}{6}$ (C) $\dfrac{5\pi}{12}$ (E) $\dfrac{5\pi}{4}$ (G) $\dfrac{5\pi}{6}$

(B) $\dfrac{5\pi}{3}$ (D) $\dfrac{9\pi}{5}$ (F) $\dfrac{7\pi}{3}$ (H) $\dfrac{7\pi}{12}$

1.10. Find the volume of the solid generated by revolving the region bounded by $y = \sqrt{x}$, $x = 0$, and $y = 1$ about the line $y = -1$.

(A) $\dfrac{7\pi}{6}$ (C) $\dfrac{5\pi}{12}$ (E) $\dfrac{5\pi}{4}$ (G) $\dfrac{5\pi}{6}$

(B) $\dfrac{5\pi}{3}$ (D) $\dfrac{9\pi}{5}$ (F) $\dfrac{7\pi}{3}$ (H) $\dfrac{7\pi}{12}$

Shell in y

Radius
$r = y^2 - 0$
$r = y^2$

Height
$ht = y + 1$

$V_{Shell} = 2\pi \int_0^1 y^2 (y+1) dy$

$V = 2\pi \int_0^1 (y^3 + y^2) dy$

$V = 2\pi \left(\dfrac{y^4}{4} + \dfrac{y^3}{3} \right) \Big|_0^1$

$V = 2\pi \left(\dfrac{1}{4} + \dfrac{1}{3} \right)$

$V = 2\pi \left(\dfrac{4+3}{12} \right)$

$V = 2\pi \left(\dfrac{7}{12} \right)$

$\boxed{V = \dfrac{7\pi}{6} \text{ units}^3}$

Washer in x

Outer Radius
$R(x) = 2$

Inner radius
$r(x) = 1 + \sqrt{x}$

$V_{washer} = \pi \int_a^b \left((R(x))^2 - (r(x))^2 \right) dx$

$V = \pi \int_0^1 (2^2 - (1+\sqrt{x})^2) dx$

$V = \pi \int_0^1 (4 - (1 + 2\sqrt{x} + x)) dx$

$V = \pi \int_0^1 (3 - 2x^{1/2} - x) dx$

$V = \pi \left[3x - 2 \cdot \dfrac{2}{3} x^{3/2} - \dfrac{x^2}{2} \right]_0^1$

$V = \pi \left[(3 - \dfrac{4}{3} - \dfrac{1}{2}) - 0 \right]$

$V = \pi \left[\dfrac{18 - 8 - 3}{6} \right]$

$\boxed{V = \dfrac{7\pi}{6} \text{ units}^3}$

1.11. Find the volume of the solid generated by revolving the region bounded by $y = \sqrt{x}\left(x^2 + 16\right)^{1/4}$, $x = 3$ and $y = 0$, about the x – axis. See the graph below.

(A) $\dfrac{17\pi}{3}$ (C) $\dfrac{23\pi}{3}$ (E) $\dfrac{61\pi}{3}$ (G) $\dfrac{67\pi}{3}$

(B) $\dfrac{19\pi}{3}$ (D) $\dfrac{53\pi}{3}$ (F) $\dfrac{47\pi}{3}$ (H) $\dfrac{81\pi}{2}$

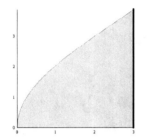

1.11. Find the volume of the solid generated by revolving the region bounded by $y = \sqrt{x}\left(x^2 + 16\right)^{1/4}$, $x = 3$ and $y = 0$, about the x – axis. See the graph below.

(A) $\dfrac{17\pi}{3}$

(C) $\dfrac{23\pi}{3}$

(E) $\dfrac{61\pi}{3}$

(G) $\dfrac{67\pi}{3}$

(B) $\dfrac{19\pi}{3}$

(D) $\dfrac{53\pi}{3}$

(F) $\dfrac{47\pi}{3}$

(H) $\dfrac{81\pi}{2}$

$$V_{disk} = \pi \int_a^b \left(r(x)\right)^2 dx$$

$$V = \pi \int_0^3 \left(\sqrt{x}(x^2+16)^{1/4}\right)^2 dx$$

$$V = \pi \int_0^3 x \cdot \sqrt{x^2+16}\ dx$$

$$V = \frac{\pi}{3}\left(x^2+16\right)^{3/2}\Big|_0^3$$

$$V = \frac{\pi}{3}\left[(9+16)^{3/2} - 16^{3/2}\right]$$

$$V = \frac{\pi}{3}(125 - 64)$$

$$\boxed{V = \frac{61\pi}{3}\ units^3}$$

DISK
inX

radius $= \sqrt{x}\,(x^2+16)^{1/4}$

$u = x^2 + 16$
$du = 2x\,dx$
$\frac{1}{2}du = x\,dx$
$\frac{1}{2}\int u^{1/2}\,du$
$\frac{1}{2}\cdot\frac{2}{3}u^{3/2}$

$25^{3/2} = \left(\sqrt{25}\right)^3$
$= 5^3$
$= 125$

$16^{3/2} = \left(\sqrt{16}\right)^3$
$= 4^3$
$= 64$

1.12. Find the x – value of the point P on $y = \dfrac{2}{3}x^{3/2}$ to the right of the

y – axis so that the length of the curve from $(0,0)$ to P is $\dfrac{52}{3}$.

(A) 8   (C) 9   (E) 6   (G) 21

(B) 2   (D) 4   (F) 15   (H) 27

1.12. Find the x – value of the point P on $y = \dfrac{2}{3}x^{3/2}$ to the right of the

y – axis so that the length of the curve from $(0,0)$ to P is $\dfrac{52}{3}$.

(A) 8   (C) 9   (E) 6   (G) 21

(B) 2   (D) 4   (F) 15   (H) 27

$$\text{Arc length} = \int_a^b \sqrt{1+(y')^2}\, dx$$

$$\frac{52}{3} = \int_0^b \sqrt{1+x}\, dx$$

$$\frac{52}{3} = \left[\frac{2}{3}(1+x)^{3/2} \Big|_0^b \right]$$

$$\frac{52}{3} = \frac{2}{3}\left[(1+b)^{3/2} - 1\right]$$

$$\frac{52}{3} \cdot \frac{3}{2} = (1+b)^{3/2} - 1$$

$$26 + 1 = (1+b)^{3/2}$$

$$27^{2/3} = 1+b$$

$$(27^{1/3})^2 = 1+b$$

$$3^2 - 1 = b$$

$$\Rightarrow \boxed{b = 8}$$

$$y = \frac{2}{3}x^{3/2}$$

$$y' = \frac{2}{3}\cdot\frac{3}{2}x^{1/2} = \sqrt{x}$$

$$(y')^2 = x$$

$$1 + (y')^2 = 1+x$$

28

1.13. Find the arclength of the curve $y = \left(4 - x^{2/3}\right)^{3/2}$ for $1 \le x \le 8$.

(A) 8   (C) 9   (E) 6   (G) 21

(B) 2   (D) 4   (F) 15   (H) 27

1.13. Find the arclength of the curve $y = \left(4 - x^{2/3}\right)^{3/2}$ for $1 \le x \le 8$.

(A) 8   (C) 9   (E) 6   (G) 21

(B) 2   (D) 4   (F) 15   (H) 27

$$\text{Arclength} = \int_a^b \sqrt{1+(y'(x))^2}\, dx$$

$$AL = \int_1^8 2x^{-1/3}\, dx$$

$$AL = \left[2 \cdot \frac{x^{2/3}}{2/3}\right]_1^8$$

$$AL = 2 \cdot \frac{3}{2}\left[8^{2/3} - 1\right]$$

$$AL = 3\left[(8^{1/3})^2 - 1\right]$$

$$AL = 3\left[2^2 - 1\right]$$

$$AL = 3 \cdot 3$$

$$\boxed{AL = 9 \text{ units}}$$

$$y = (4 - x^{2/3})^{3/2}$$

$$y' = \frac{3}{2}(4 - x^{2/3})^{1/2} \cdot -\frac{2}{3}x^{-1/3}$$

$$y' = \frac{-\sqrt{4 - x^{2/3}}}{x^{1/3}}$$

$$(y')^2 = \frac{4 - x^{2/3}}{x^{2/3}}$$

$$(y')^2 = \frac{4}{x^{2/3}} - 1$$

$$1 + (y')^2 = 1 + \left(\frac{4}{x^{2/3}} - 1\right)$$

$$1 + (y')^2 = \frac{4}{x^{2/3}}$$

$$\sqrt{1 + (y')^2} = \sqrt{\frac{4}{x^{2/3}}} = \frac{2}{x^{1/3}}$$

1.14. Find the length of the curve given by $x = \dfrac{y^3}{12} + \dfrac{1}{y}$, for $1 \le y \le 2$.

(A) $\dfrac{\pi}{12}$ (C) $\dfrac{1}{12}$ (E) $\dfrac{\pi}{2}$ (G) $\dfrac{5}{12}$

(B) $\dfrac{13}{12}$ (D) $\dfrac{1}{2}$ (F) 2 (H) $\dfrac{17}{12}$

1.14. Find the length of the curve given by $x = \dfrac{y^3}{12} + \dfrac{1}{y}$, for $1 \le y \le 2$.

(A) $\dfrac{\pi}{12}$ (C) $\dfrac{1}{12}$ (E) $\dfrac{\pi}{2}$ (G) $\dfrac{5}{12}$

(B) $\dfrac{13}{12}$ (D) $\dfrac{1}{2}$ (F) 2 (H) $\dfrac{17}{12}$

$\text{Arclength} = \displaystyle\int_a^b \sqrt{1 + (x'(y))^2}\, dy$

$x = \dfrac{y^3}{12} + \dfrac{1}{y}$ so $x' = \dfrac{3y^2}{12} - \dfrac{1}{y^2} = \dfrac{y^2}{4} - \dfrac{1}{y^2}$

Thus $(x')^2 = \left(\dfrac{y^2}{4} - \dfrac{1}{y^2}\right)\left(\dfrac{y^2}{4} - \dfrac{1}{y^2}\right)$

$(x')^2 = \dfrac{y^4}{16} - \dfrac{1}{4} - \dfrac{1}{4} + \dfrac{1}{y^4}$

$(x')^2 = \dfrac{y^4}{16} - \dfrac{1}{2} + \dfrac{1}{y^4} = \left(\dfrac{y^2}{4} - \dfrac{1}{y^2}\right)^2$

Now add 1

$1 + (x')^2 = \dfrac{y^4}{16}\left[-\dfrac{1}{2} + 1\right] + \dfrac{1}{y^4}$

$1 + (x')^2 = \dfrac{y^4}{16} + \dfrac{1}{2} + \dfrac{1}{y^4} = \left(\dfrac{y^2}{4} + \dfrac{1}{y^2}\right)^2$

If $1 + (x')^2 = \left(\dfrac{y^2}{4} + \dfrac{1}{y^2}\right)^2$, then $\sqrt{1+(x')^2} = \dfrac{y^2}{4} + \dfrac{1}{y^2}$

Finally integrate to find the arclength:

$A.L = \displaystyle\int_1^2 \left(\dfrac{y^2}{4} + \dfrac{1}{y^2}\right) dy = \int_1^2 \left(\dfrac{y^2}{4} + y^{-2}\right) dy$

$A.L = \left[\dfrac{y^3}{12} - \dfrac{1}{y}\right]_1^2 = \left(\dfrac{8}{12} - \dfrac{1}{2}\right) - \left(\dfrac{1}{12} - 1\right)$

$A.L = \dfrac{7}{12} - \dfrac{1}{2} + 1 = \dfrac{7 - 6 + 12}{12}$

$\boxed{A.L = \dfrac{13}{12} \text{ units}}$

1.15. Find the area of the surface generated by revolving the curve $x = \sqrt{9 - y^2}$ for $-1 \le y \le 1$ about the y – axis.

(A) 2π (C) 4π (E) 8π (G) 12π

(B) π (D) 24π (F) 36π (H) 15π

1.15. Find the area of the surface generated by revolving the curve $x = \sqrt{9 - y^2}$ for $-1 \le y \le 1$ about the y – axis.

(A) 2π (C) 4π (E) 8π (G) 12π

(B) π (D) 24π (F) 36π (H) 15π

Surface Area for a curve rotated about y-axis $SA = \int 2\pi x \, ds$

We are given y-bounds and the function is given as $x = g(y)$ } Do the integral in y

$$SA = 2\pi \int_a^b \underbrace{\sqrt{9-y^2}}_{x} \sqrt{1 + (x'(y))^2} \, dy = 2\pi \int_{-1}^{1} \sqrt{9-y^2} \cdot \frac{3}{\sqrt{9-y^2}} \, dy$$

$x = \sqrt{9-y^2}$

Find $x'(y)$

$x' = \frac{1}{2\sqrt{9-y^2}} \cdot (-2y) = \frac{-y}{\sqrt{9-y^2}}$

Now square x'

$(x')^2 = \frac{y^2}{9-y^2}$

Next add 1

$1 + (x')^2 = 1 + \frac{y^2}{9-y^2}$

$1+(x')^2 = \frac{9-y^2+y^2}{9-y^2} = \frac{9}{9-y^2}$

Lastly take $\sqrt{}$

$$\boxed{\sqrt{1+(x')^2} = \frac{3}{\sqrt{9-y^2}}}$$

$$SA = 2\pi \int_{-1}^{1} 3 \, dy$$

$$SA = 6\pi \, [y]_{-1}^{1}$$

$$SA = 6\pi \, (1 - (-1))$$

$$\boxed{SA = 12\pi \text{ units}^2}$$

1.16. Find the area of the surface generated by revolving the

curve $y = \dfrac{1}{3}\left(x^2 + 2\right)^{3/2}$ for $0 \le x \le \sqrt{6}$ about the y – axis.

(A) $6\pi\sqrt{6}$ (C) 67π (E) $12\pi\sqrt{6}$ (G) 24π

(B) $3\pi\sqrt{6}$ (D) 12π (F) 36π (H) 6π

1.16. Find the area of the surface generated by revolving the curve $y = \dfrac{1}{3}\left(x^2 + 2\right)^{3/2}$ for $0 \le x \le \sqrt{6}$ about the y – axis.

(A) $6\pi\sqrt{6}$ (C) 67π (E) $12\pi\sqrt{6}$ (G) 24π

(B) $3\pi\sqrt{6}$ (D) 12π (F) 36π (H) 6π

$$\left.\begin{array}{l}\text{Surface area}\\\text{generated by}\\\text{rotating a curve}\\\text{about the }y\text{-axis}\end{array}\right\} \quad SA = 2\pi \int x\, ds$$

$$\left.\begin{array}{l}\text{we are given } x \text{ bounds}\\\text{and the function is}\\\text{given as } y = f(x)\end{array}\right\} \quad \text{Do the integral in } x$$

$$SA = 2\pi \int_a^b x \cdot \sqrt{1 + (y'(x))^2}\; dx = 2\pi \int_0^{\sqrt{6}} x \cdot (x^2 + 1)\, dx$$

$$y = \tfrac{1}{3}(x^2 + 2)^{3/2}$$

$$SA = 2\pi \int_0^{\sqrt{6}} (x^3 + x)\, dx$$

$$\underline{\text{Find } y'}$$

$$y' = \tfrac{1}{3} \cdot \tfrac{3}{2} (x^2 + 2)^{1/2} \cdot \underset{\text{Chain Rule}}{2x} = x\sqrt{x^2 + 2}$$

$$SA = 2\pi\left[\tfrac{x^4}{4} + \tfrac{x^2}{2}\right]_0^{\sqrt{6}}$$

$$\underline{\text{Now square}}$$

$$(y')^2 = \left[x(x^2+2)^{1/2}\right]^2 = x^2(x^2 + 2)$$

$$SA = 2\pi\left[\left(\tfrac{36}{4} + \tfrac{6}{2}\right) - 0\right]$$

$$(y')^2 = x^4 + 2x^2$$

$$SA = 2\pi(9 + 3)$$

$$\underline{\text{Now add 1}}$$

$$1 + (y')^2 = x^4 + 2x^2 + 1$$

$$\boxed{SA = 24\pi \; \text{units}^2}$$

$$1 + (y')^2 = (x^2 + 1)(x^2 + 1) = (x^2 + 1)^2$$

$$\underline{\text{Finally take } \sqrt{\ }}$$

$$\sqrt{1 + (y')^2} = x^2 + 1$$

1.17. Find the surface area generated by revolving the curve $y = \sqrt{3x+1}$ for $1 \leq x \leq 3$ about the x – axis.

(A) $\dfrac{74\pi}{5}$ (C) $\dfrac{97\pi}{12}$ (E) $\dfrac{124\pi}{15}$ (G) $\dfrac{224\pi}{15}$

(B) $\dfrac{115\pi}{9}$ (D) $\dfrac{85\pi}{6}$ (F) $\dfrac{109\pi}{9}$ (H) $\dfrac{152\pi}{5}$

1.17. Find the surface area generated by revolving the curve $y = \sqrt{3x+1}$ for $1 \le x \le 3$ about the x – axis.

(A) $\dfrac{74\pi}{5}$ (C) $\dfrac{97\pi}{12}$ (E) $\dfrac{124\pi}{15}$ (G) $\dfrac{224\pi}{15}$

(B) $\dfrac{115\pi}{9}$ (D) $\dfrac{85\pi}{6}$ (F) $\dfrac{109\pi}{9}$ (H) $\dfrac{152\pi}{5}$

Surface area generated
be revolving a curve
about the x-axis $\Bigg\}$ $SA = 2\pi \int_a^b y \, ds$

we are given x-bounds
and the function is
given as a $y = f(x)$ $\Bigg\}$ Do the integral
in X

$$SA = 2\pi \int_1^3 \underbrace{\sqrt{3x+1}}_{y} \sqrt{1+(y'(x))^2} \, dx = 2\pi \int_1^3 \sqrt{3x+1} \cdot \frac{\sqrt{12x+13}}{2\sqrt{3x+1}} \, dx$$

$y = \sqrt{3x+1}$

Find y'

$y' = \dfrac{1}{2\sqrt{3x+1}} \cdot 3 = \dfrac{3}{2\sqrt{3x+1}}$

Now square y'

$(y')^2 = \dfrac{9}{4(3x+1)} = \dfrac{9}{12x+4}$

Next add 1

$1+(y')^2 = 1 + \dfrac{9}{12x+4} = \dfrac{12x+4+9}{12x+4}$

$1+(y')^2 = \dfrac{12x+13}{12x+4} = \dfrac{12x+13}{4(3x+1)}$

Finally, take $\sqrt{}$

$$\boxed{\sqrt{1+(y')^2} = \dfrac{\sqrt{12x+13}}{2\sqrt{3x+1}}}$$

$$SA = \pi \int_1^3 \sqrt{12x+13} \, dx$$

$u = 12x+13$

$\dfrac{du}{12} = \dfrac{12 \, dx}{12}$

$\dfrac{1}{12} du = dx$

$\dfrac{1}{12} \int \sqrt{u} \, du$

$\dfrac{1}{12} \cdot \dfrac{u^{3/2}}{\frac{3}{2}} = \dfrac{1}{18} u^{3/2}$

49
$\times 7$
$\underline{343}$ 13
-125
$\overline{218}$

$$SA = \dfrac{\pi}{18}\left[(12x+13)^{3/2}\right]_1^3$$

$$SA = \dfrac{\pi}{18}\left[49^{3/2} - 25^{3/2}\right]$$

$$SA = \dfrac{\pi}{18}\left[7^3 - 5^3\right]$$

$$SA = \dfrac{\pi}{18}\left[343 - 125\right]$$

$$SA = \dfrac{\pi}{18}\overset{109}{(\cancel{218})} \atop 9$$

$$\boxed{SA = \dfrac{109\pi}{9} \text{ units}^2}$$

1.18. Find the y coordinate of the center of mass of the lamina with constant density ρ bounded above by the graph of $y = 4 - x^2$ and bounded below by the graph of $y = x + 2$ given the fact that the total mass $M = \dfrac{9\rho}{2}$.

(A) $\dfrac{-1}{2}$

(C) $\dfrac{16}{3}$

(E) $\dfrac{12}{5}$

(G) $\dfrac{32}{15}$

(B) $\dfrac{8}{3}$

(D) $\dfrac{24}{5}$

(F) $\dfrac{22}{3}$

(H) $\dfrac{64}{15}$

1.18. Find the y coordinate of the center of mass of the lamina with constant density ρ bounded above by the graph of $y = 4 - x^2$ and bounded below by the graph of $y = x + 2$ given the fact that the total mass $M = \dfrac{9\rho}{2}$.

(A) $\dfrac{-1}{2}$

(C) $\dfrac{16}{3}$

(E) $\dfrac{12}{5}$

(G) $\dfrac{32}{15}$

(B) $\dfrac{8}{3}$

(D) $\dfrac{24}{5}$

(F) $\dfrac{22}{3}$

(H) $\dfrac{64}{15}$

$y = 4 - x^2$

$y = x + 2$

$\bar{y} = \dfrac{M_x}{M} = \dfrac{\frac{54\rho}{5}}{\frac{9\rho}{2}} = \dfrac{54\rho}{5} \cdot \dfrac{2}{9\rho}$

$4 - x^2 = x + 2$

$0 = x^2 + x - 2$

$0 = (x+2)(x-1)$

$x = -2 \quad x = 1$

$\boxed{\bar{y} = \dfrac{12}{5}}$

$\underset{\text{upper}}{} \quad \underset{\text{lower}}{}$

$M_x = \dfrac{1}{2} \int_a^b \rho \cdot \left[[F(x)]^2 - [g(x)]^2 \right] dx$

$M_x = \dfrac{\rho}{2} \int_{-2}^{1} \left[(4-x^2)^2 - (x+2)^2 \right] dx$

$M_x = \dfrac{\rho}{2} \int_{-2}^{1} \left[16 - 8x^2 + x^4 - (x^2 + 4x + 4) \right] dx$

$M_x = \dfrac{\rho}{2} \int_{-2}^{1} (x^4 - 9x^2 - 4x + 12) \, dx$

$= \dfrac{\rho}{2} \left[\dfrac{x^5}{5} - 3x^3 - 2x^2 + 12x \right]_{-2}^{1}$

$= \dfrac{\rho}{2} \left[\left(\dfrac{1}{5} - 3 - 2 + 12 \right) - \left(\dfrac{-32}{5} + 24 - 8 - 24 \right) \right]$

$= \dfrac{\rho}{2} \left[\dfrac{1}{5} + 7 + \dfrac{32}{5} + 8 \right]$

$M_x = \dfrac{\rho}{2} \left[\dfrac{33}{5} + 15 \right] = \dfrac{33 + 75}{5} \cdot \dfrac{\rho}{2} = \dfrac{108 \rho}{10}$

$M_x = \dfrac{54}{5} \rho$

1.19. Find the x coordinate of the centroid (center of mass) of the triangular region with vertices $(0,0)$, $(0,4)$, and $(6,0)$.

(A) 1   (C) 3   (E) $\dfrac{5}{2}$ (G) $\dfrac{7}{4}$

(B) 2   (D) $\dfrac{4}{3}$ (F) $\dfrac{9}{4}$ (H) $\dfrac{3}{2}$

1.19. Find the x coordinate of the centroid (center of mass) of the triangular region with vertices $(0,0)$, $(0,4)$, and $(6,0)$.

(A) 1   (C) 3   (E) $\dfrac{5}{2}$ (G) $\dfrac{7}{4}$

(B) 2   (D) $\dfrac{4}{3}$ (F) $\dfrac{9}{4}$ (H) $\dfrac{3}{2}$

Assume constant density ρ

$y = -\frac{2}{3}x + 4$

$\bar{x} = \dfrac{M_y}{Mass}$

$Mass = \int_a^b \rho \cdot f(x)\, dx$

$Mass = \rho \int_0^6 \left(-\frac{2}{3}x + 4\right) dx$

$\underbrace{\qquad\qquad\qquad}_{\substack{\text{area of the}\\\text{triangle}}}$

$Mass = \rho \cdot \frac{1}{2}(base)(height)$

$Mass = \frac{\rho}{2}(6)(4) = 12\rho$

$M_y = \rho \int_a^b x \cdot f(x)\, dx = \rho \int_0^6 x\left(-\frac{2}{3}x + 4\right) dx = \rho \int_0^6 \left(-\frac{2}{3}x^2 + 4x\right) dx$

$M_y = \rho \left[-\frac{2}{3} \cdot \frac{x^3}{3} + 4\frac{x^2}{2}\right]_0^6 = \rho \left(-\frac{2}{9}x^3 + 2x^2\right)\Big|_0^6$

$M_y = \rho \left[-\frac{2}{9}(216) + 2 \cdot 36\right] = \rho\left[-2(24) + 2 \cdot 36\right]$

$M_y = \rho\left[-48 + 72\right] = 24\rho$

$\bar{x} = \dfrac{24\rho}{12\rho} \qquad \boxed{\bar{x} = 2}$

1.20. Consider the region bounded by $y = x, y = \sin x,$ and $x = \pi$.

If the density is given by $\rho(x) = 2x$, find the moment about the y – axis.

1.20. Consider the region bounded by $y = x$, $y = \sin x$, and $x = \pi$.

If the density is given by $\rho(x) = 2x$, find the moment about the $y-$axis.

$$M_y = \int_a^b \rho(x) \cdot x \cdot \left[\,\overset{\text{upper}}{\overset{\downarrow}{f(x)}} - \overset{\text{lower}}{\overset{\downarrow}{g(x)}}\,\right] dx$$

$$M_y = \int_0^\pi 2x \cdot x \left[x - \sin x\right] dx$$

$$M_y = \int_0^\pi \left(2x^3 - 2x^2 \sin x\right) dx \quad \overset{\text{Integration by parts, but}}{}$$

we can use
the shortcut

$$M_y = \left[\frac{x^4}{2} + 2x^2\cos x - 4x\sin x - 4\cos x\right]_0^\pi$$

D	I
$-2x^2$	$\sin x$
$-4x$	$-\cos x$
-4	$-\sin x$
0	$\cos x$

$$M_y = \left(\frac{\pi^4}{2} + 2\pi^2 \cos\pi - 4\sin\pi - 4\cos\pi\right) - \left(-4\cos 0\right)$$

$$M_y = \frac{\pi^4}{2} - 2\pi^2 + 4 + 4$$

$$\boxed{M_y = \frac{\pi^4}{2} - 2\pi^2 + 8}$$

44

1.21 Evaluate the integral

$$\int_0^4 x^2 e^{\frac{x}{2}} dx$$

(A) $\frac{1}{3}\left(\sqrt{e}-1\right)$ (C) $8\left(e^2-2\right)$ (E) $16\left(e^2-1\right)$

(B) $\sqrt{e}+1$ (D) $16\left(e^2-10\right)$ (F) $8e-16$

1.21 Evaluate the integral

$$\int_0^4 x^2 e^{\frac{x}{2}} dx$$

(A) $\frac{1}{3}\left(\sqrt{e}-1\right)$ (C) $8\left(e^2-2\right)$ (E) $16\left(e^2-1\right)$

(B) $\sqrt{e}+1$ (D) $16\left(e^2-10\right)$ (F) $8e-16$

Integration by parts twice
or use the shortcut

D	I
x^2 ⊕	$e^{x/2}$
$2x$ ⊖	$2e^{x/2}$
2 ⊕	$4e^{x/2}$
0	$8e^{x/2}$

$$\int e^{Kx}dx = \frac{1}{K}e^{Kx}+c$$

$$= \left[2x^2e^{x/2} - 8xe^{x/2} + 16e^{x/2}\right]_0^4$$

$$= 2\left[e^{x/2}\left(x^2-4x+8\right)\right]_0^4$$

$$= 2\left[e^2(16-16+8) - 1\cdot(0-0+8)\right]$$

$$= 2\left[8e^2 - 8\right] = \boxed{16\left(e^2-1\right)}$$

46

1.22 Evaluate the integral

$$\int_0^1 x^2 \arctan(x)\,dx$$

(A) $\dfrac{\pi}{4} + \dfrac{1}{12}\ln 4$

(B) $\dfrac{\pi}{12} - \dfrac{1}{6} + \dfrac{1}{6}\ln 2$

(C) $\dfrac{1}{12} + \ln 2$

(D) $\dfrac{\pi}{3} + \dfrac{1}{3}\ln 2$

(E) $\dfrac{\pi}{6} + \dfrac{1}{6}\ln 4$

(F) $\dfrac{\pi}{12} + \dfrac{1}{6}\ln 2$

1.22 Evaluate the integral

$$\int_0^1 x^2 \arctan(x)\,dx$$

(A) $\dfrac{\pi}{4} + \dfrac{1}{12}\ln 4$

(C) $\dfrac{1}{12} + \ln 2$

(E) $\dfrac{\pi}{6} + \dfrac{1}{6}\ln 4$

(B) $\dfrac{\pi}{12} - \dfrac{1}{6} + \dfrac{1}{6}\ln 2$

(D) $\dfrac{\pi}{3} + \dfrac{1}{3}\ln 2$

(F) $\dfrac{\pi}{12} + \dfrac{1}{6}\ln 2$

Use Integration by Parts
  but you can't use the shortcut

$$u = \arctan x \qquad dv = x^2$$

$$du = \frac{1}{1+x^2}\,dx \qquad v = \frac{x^3}{3}$$

$$uv - \int v\,du$$

$$= \frac{x^3}{3}\arctan x - \frac{1}{3}\int \frac{x^3}{1+x^2}\,dx$$

use LongDivision

$$x^2+1 \overline{\smash{\big)}\, x^3}$$
$$\underline{-(x^3+x)}$$
$$-x$$

$$= \frac{x^3}{3}\arctan x - \frac{1}{3}\int\left(x - \frac{x}{x^2+1}\right)dx$$

$$= \frac{x^3}{3}\arctan x - \frac{1}{3}\left[\frac{x^2}{2} - \frac{1}{2}\ln(x^2+1)\right]\Big|_0^1$$

$$= \left(\frac{1}{3}\arctan 1 - \frac{1}{3}\left[\frac{1}{2} - \frac{1}{2}\ln 2\right]\right) - \left(0 - \frac{1}{3}[0-0]\right)$$

$$= \frac{1}{3}\cdot\frac{\pi}{4} - \frac{1}{3}\left(\frac{1}{2} - \frac{1}{2}\ln 2\right)$$

$$= \boxed{\frac{\pi}{12} - \frac{1}{6} + \frac{1}{6}\ln 2}$$

48

1.23 Evaluate the integral

$$\int_{1}^{\sqrt[3]{e}} 18x^2 \ln(x)\,dx$$

(A) $\dfrac{3}{2}$ (C) $\dfrac{5}{2}$ (E) $\dfrac{7}{2}$ (G) 1

(B) $\dfrac{1}{2}$ (D) 2   (F) 3   (H) 4

1.23 Evaluate the integral

$$\int_{1}^{\sqrt[3]{e}} 18x^2 \ln(x)dx$$

(A) $\dfrac{3}{2}$ (C) $\dfrac{5}{2}$ (E) $\dfrac{7}{2}$ (G) 1

(B) $\dfrac{1}{2}$ (D) 2   (F) 3   (H) 4

Use Integration by Parts
but you can't use the shortcut

$u = \ln x$ $dv = 18x^2$

$du = \frac{1}{x}dx$ $v = 6x^3$

$uv - \int v\,du$

$= 6x^3 \cdot \ln x - \int 6x^2 dx$

$= \left[6x^3 \cdot \ln x - 2x^3\right]\Big|_1^{\sqrt[3]{e}}$

$= \left[6\left(\sqrt[3]{e}\right)^3 \ln \sqrt[3]{e} - 2\left(\sqrt[3]{e}\right)^3\right] - (0-2)$

$= 6e \cdot \ln e^{1/3} - 2e + 2$

$= 6e \cdot \frac{1}{3} - 2e + 2$

$= 2e - 2e + 2$

$= \boxed{2}$

1.24 Evaluate the integral

$$\int_0^{\pi/6} x\sin(3x)\,dx$$

(A) $\dfrac{1}{2}$ (C) $\dfrac{1}{3}$ (E) $\dfrac{1}{4}$ (G) $\dfrac{3}{4}$

(B) $\dfrac{1}{8}$ (D) $\dfrac{1}{16}$ (F) $\dfrac{1}{9}$ (H) $\dfrac{2}{3}$

1.24 Evaluate the integral

$$\int_0^{\pi/6} x\sin(3x)\,dx$$

(A) $\dfrac{1}{2}$ (C) $\dfrac{1}{3}$ (E) $\dfrac{1}{4}$ (G) $\dfrac{3}{4}$

(B) $\dfrac{1}{8}$ (D) $\dfrac{1}{16}$ (F) $\dfrac{1}{9}$ (H) $\dfrac{2}{3}$

Use Integration by Parts Shortcut

$$
\begin{array}{ccc}
D & I & \int \sin kx\,dx \\
x & \sin(3x) & = -\tfrac{1}{k}\cos kx + c \\
1 & -\tfrac{1}{3}\cos(3x) & \\
0 & -\tfrac{1}{9}\sin(3x) &
\end{array}
$$

$$= \left[-\frac{x}{3}\cos(3x) + \frac{1}{9}\sin(3x) \right]_0^{\pi/6}$$

$$= \left(-\frac{\pi}{18}\cos(\pi/2) + \frac{1}{9}\sin\left(\frac{\pi}{2}\right) \right) - (0+0)$$

$$= \boxed{\frac{1}{9}}$$

Anti-deriv. w/o Shortcut:

$u = x \qquad dv = \sin(3x)$

$du = dx \qquad v = -\tfrac{1}{3}\cos(3x)$

$$uv - \int v\,du$$

$$= -\frac{1}{3}x\cdot\cos(3x) + \frac{1}{3}\int \cos(3x)\,dx$$

$$= -\frac{1}{3}x\cos(3x) + \frac{1}{3}\cdot\frac{1}{3}\sin(3x)$$

$$= -\frac{1}{3}x\cos(3x) + \frac{1}{9}\sin(3x)$$

1.25 Evaluate the integral

$$\int_0^4 x^2 \cos\left(\frac{\pi}{2}x\right) dx$$

(A) $\dfrac{4}{\pi} - \dfrac{16}{\pi^3}$

(C) $\dfrac{64}{\pi^2}$

(E) $\dfrac{-16}{\pi^2}$

(G) $\dfrac{16}{\pi^2}$

(B) $\dfrac{8}{\pi} + \dfrac{16}{\pi^3}$

(D) $\dfrac{8}{\pi}$

(F) $\dfrac{8}{\pi^2}$

(H) $\dfrac{32}{\pi^2}$

1.25 Evaluate the integral

$$\int_0^4 x^2 \cos\left(\frac{\pi}{2}x\right) dx$$

(A) $\dfrac{4}{\pi} - \dfrac{16}{\pi^3}$ (C) $\dfrac{64}{\pi^2}$ (E) $\dfrac{-16}{\pi^2}$ (G) $\dfrac{16}{\pi^2}$

(B) $\dfrac{8}{\pi} + \dfrac{16}{\pi^3}$ (D) $\dfrac{8}{\pi}$ (F) $\dfrac{8}{\pi^2}$ (H) $\dfrac{32}{\pi^2}$

Use Integration by Parts
(a) with the shortcut
(b) without the shortcut

(a)

$$\begin{array}{ll}
D & \\
x^2 & \oplus \cos\frac{\pi}{2}x \\
2x & \ominus \frac{2}{\pi}\sin\frac{\pi}{2}x \\
2 & \oplus -\frac{4}{\pi^2}\cos\frac{\pi}{2}x \\
0 & \ominus -\frac{8}{\pi^3}\sin(\frac{\pi}{2}x)
\end{array}$$

$$= \frac{2x^2}{\pi}\sin\frac{\pi}{2}x + \frac{8x}{\pi^2}\cos\frac{\pi}{2}x - \frac{16}{\pi^3}\sin\frac{\pi}{2}x$$

(b) $\quad u = x^2 \qquad dv = \cos\frac{\pi}{2}x$
$\qquad du = 2dx \qquad v = \frac{2}{\pi}\sin\frac{\pi}{2}x$

$= uv - \int v\,du$

$= \frac{2x^2}{\pi}\sin\frac{\pi}{2}x - \frac{4}{\pi}\underbrace{\int x\sin\frac{\pi}{2}x\,dx}_{\text{I.B.P.}}$

$u = x \qquad dv = \sin\frac{\pi}{2}x$
$du = dx \qquad v = -\frac{2}{\pi}\cos\frac{\pi}{2}x$

$\Rightarrow \qquad uv - \int v\,du$

$= \frac{2x^2}{\pi}\sin\left(\frac{\pi}{2}x\right) - \frac{4}{\pi}\left[-\frac{2x}{\pi}\cos\frac{\pi}{2}x + \frac{2}{\pi}\int\cos\frac{\pi}{2}x\,dx\right]$

$\qquad\qquad\qquad\qquad\qquad \frac{2}{\pi}\left(\frac{2}{\pi}\sin\frac{\pi}{2}x\right)$

$= \frac{2x^2}{\pi}\sin\left(\frac{\pi}{2}x\right) - \frac{4}{\pi}\left[-\frac{2x}{\pi}\cos\left(\frac{\pi}{2}x\right) + \frac{4}{\pi^2}\sin\frac{\pi}{2}x\right]$

$= \frac{2x^2}{\pi}\sin\left(\frac{\pi}{2}x\right) + \frac{8x}{\pi^2}\cos\left(\frac{\pi}{2}x\right) - \frac{16}{\pi^3}\sin\left(\frac{\pi}{2}x\right)$

$= \frac{2}{\pi}\left[x^2\sin\frac{\pi}{2}x + \frac{4x}{\pi}\cos\left(\frac{\pi}{2}x\right) - \frac{8}{\pi^2}\sin\left(\frac{\pi}{2}x\right)\right]\Big|_0^4$

$= \frac{2}{\pi}\left[\left(16\sin 2\pi + \frac{16}{\pi}\cos 2\pi - \frac{8}{\pi^2}\sin 2\pi\right) - (0-0-0)\right]$

$= \frac{2}{\pi}\cdot\frac{16}{\pi} = \boxed{\dfrac{32}{\pi^2}}$

54

SECTION II

Trigonometric Integrals
Trigonometric Substitution
Partial Fraction Decomposition
Probability
Improper Integrals

2.1 Evaluate the integral

$$\int_0^{\pi/2} \sqrt{\cos x}\, \sin^3 x\, dx$$

(A) $\dfrac{11}{20}$ (C) $\dfrac{9}{20}$ (E) $\dfrac{8}{21}$ (G) $\dfrac{2}{5}$

(B) $\dfrac{3}{7}$ (D) $\dfrac{4}{11}$ (F) $\dfrac{1}{2}$ (H) $\dfrac{11}{21}$

2.1 Evaluate the integral

$$\int_0^{\pi/2} \sqrt{\cos x}\,\sin^3 x \, dx$$

(A) $\dfrac{11}{20}$ (C) $\dfrac{9}{20}$ (E) $\dfrac{8}{21}$ (G) $\dfrac{2}{5}$

(B) $\dfrac{3}{7}$ (D) $\dfrac{4}{11}$ (F) $\dfrac{1}{2}$ (H) $\dfrac{11}{21}$

<u>**Power of sinx is odd:**</u>
- factor out one power of sinx

$$= \int_0^{\pi/2} \sqrt{\cos x}\,\sin^2 x \cdot \sin x \, dx$$

- Transform remaining powers using $\sin^2 x = 1 - \cos^2 x$

$$= \int_0^{\pi/2} \sqrt{\cos x}\,(1 - \cos^2 x)\sin x \, dx$$

- Let $u = \cos x$ $x = 0 \Rightarrow u = 1$ LL

     $du = -\sin x \, dx$ $x = \frac{\pi}{2} \Rightarrow u = 0$ UL

     $-1 \cdot du = \sin x \, dx$

$$= \int_1^0 \sqrt{u}\,(1 - u^2) \cdot -1 \cdot du \qquad LL > UL$$

$$= -\int_0^1 (\sqrt{u} - u^{5/2}) \cdot -1 \, du$$

$$= \int_0^1 (u^{1/2} - u^{5/2}) \, du = \left[\frac{2}{3}u^{3/2} - \frac{2u^{7/2}}{7} \right]_0^1$$

$$= \left(\frac{2}{3} - \frac{2}{7}\right) - 0 = \frac{14 - 6}{21} = \boxed{\frac{8}{21}}$$

60

2.2 Evaluate the integral

$$\int_{0}^{\pi/6} \sin^3(3x)\,dx$$

(A) $\dfrac{1}{3}$ (C) $\dfrac{2}{9}$ (E) $\dfrac{1}{9}$ (G) $\dfrac{5}{3}$

(B) $\dfrac{7}{9}$ (D) $\dfrac{4}{9}$ (F) $\dfrac{4}{3}$ (H) $\dfrac{2}{3}$

2.2 Evaluate the integral

$$\int_0^{\pi/6} \sin^3(3x)\,dx$$

(A) $\dfrac{1}{3}$ (C) $\dfrac{2}{9}$ (E) $\dfrac{1}{9}$ (G) $\dfrac{5}{3}$

(B) $\dfrac{7}{9}$ (D) $\dfrac{4}{9}$ (F) $\dfrac{4}{3}$ (H) $\dfrac{2}{3}$

Power of $\sin(3x)$ is odd

• factor out one power of $\sin(3x)$

$$= \int_0^{\pi/6} \sin^2(3x) \cdot \sin(3x)\,dx$$

• transform remaining powers of $\sin(3x)$
 by $\sin^2(3x) = 1 - \cos^2(3x)$

$$= \int_0^{\pi/6} (1 - \cos^2(3x))\,\sin(3x)\,dx$$

• let $u = \cos(3x)$
  $du = -3\sin(3x)\,dx$
  $-\frac{1}{3}du = \sin(3x)\,dx$

$$\int (1-u^2) \cdot -\tfrac{1}{3}\,du = +\tfrac{1}{3}\int (u^2-1)\,du$$

$$= \tfrac{1}{3}\left(u^{3}/_3 - u\right)$$

$$= \tfrac{1}{3}\left[\tfrac{1}{3}\cos^3(3x) - \cos(3x)\right]_0^{\pi/6}$$

$$= \tfrac{1}{3}\left[\left(\tfrac{1}{3}\underbrace{\cos\tfrac{\pi}{2}}_{0}\right)^3 - \underbrace{\cos\tfrac{\pi}{2}}_{0} - \left(\tfrac{1}{3}\cdot 1 - 1\right)\right]$$

$$= \tfrac{1}{3}\left[-\left(-\tfrac{2}{3}\right)\right] = \boxed{\dfrac{2}{9}}$$

2.3 Evaluate the integral

$$\int_{0}^{\pi} 40 \sin^4(x)\,dx$$

(A) $\dfrac{\pi}{4}$ (C) 3π (E) 5 (G) $\dfrac{5\pi}{3}$

(B) $\dfrac{4\pi}{3}$ (D) 15π (F) 4π (H) 45π

2.3 Evaluate the integral

$$\int_{0}^{\pi} 40\sin^4(x)\,dx$$

(A) $\dfrac{\pi}{4}$ (C) 3π (E) 5 (G) $\dfrac{5\pi}{3}$

(B) $\dfrac{4\pi}{3}$ (D) 15π (F) 4π (H) 45π

Only power present even:

- use $\sin^2 x = \frac{1}{2}(1-\cos 2x)$ $\cos^2 x = \frac{1}{2}(1+\cos 2x)$
  to transform all even powers of $\sin x$

$$\sin^4 x = \sin^2 x \cdot \sin^2 x$$
$$\sin^4 x = \frac{1}{2}(1-\cos 2x)\frac{1}{2}(1-\cos 2x)$$
$$\sin^4 x = \frac{1}{4}(1 - 2\cos 2x + \cos^2 2x)$$
$$\sin^4 x = \frac{1}{4}\left(1 - 2\cos 2x + \frac{1}{2}(1+\cos 4x)\right)$$
$$\sin^4 x = \frac{1}{4}\left(1 - 2\cos 2x + \frac{1}{2} + \frac{1}{2}\cos 4x\right)$$
$$\sin^4 x = \frac{1}{4}\left(\frac{3}{2} - 2\cos 2x + \frac{1}{2}\cos 4x\right)$$

$$= 40\int_{0}^{\pi} \frac{1}{4}\left(\frac{3}{2} - 2\cos 2x + \frac{1}{2}\cos 4x\right) dx$$

$$= 10\left[\int_{0}^{\pi}\frac{3}{2}\,dx - \underbrace{\int_{0}^{\pi} 2\cos 2x\,dx}_{\substack{0 \text{ since it} \\ \text{is a full} \\ \text{period of} \\ \cos 2x}} + \underbrace{\int_{0}^{\pi}\frac{1}{2}\cos 4x\,dx}_{\substack{0 \text{ since it} \\ \text{is 2 full periods} \\ \text{of } \cos 4x}}\right]$$

$$= 15\int_{0}^{\pi} dx = 15[x]_{0}^{\pi} = \boxed{15\pi}$$

2.4 Evaluate the integral

$$\int_{0}^{\pi/3} \tan^3(x)\sec^3(x)\,dx$$

(A) $\dfrac{58}{15}$ (C) $\dfrac{7}{3}$ (E) $\dfrac{14}{3}$ (G) $\dfrac{46}{15}$

(B) $\dfrac{31}{5}$ (D) $\dfrac{52}{5}$ (F) $\dfrac{62}{5}$ (H) $\dfrac{93}{12}$

2.4 Evaluate the integral

$$\int_0^{\pi/3} \tan^3(x)\sec^3(x)\, dx$$

(A) $\dfrac{58}{15}$ (C) $\dfrac{7}{3}$ (E) $\dfrac{14}{3}$ (G) $\dfrac{46}{15}$

(B) $\dfrac{31}{5}$ (D) $\dfrac{52}{5}$ (F) $\dfrac{62}{5}$ (H) $\dfrac{93}{12}$

<u>Power of tanx odd with secx powers present:</u>

• Factor out tanx·secx

$$= \int_0^{\pi/3} \tan^2 x \cdot \sec^2 x \cdot \tan x \sec x \, dx$$

• Transform remaining even power
  of tanx using
  $$\tan^2 x = \sec^2 x - 1$$

$$= \int_0^{\pi/3} (\sec^2 x - 1)\sec^2 x \tan x \sec x \, dx$$

• Let $u = \sec x$
  $$du = \sec x \tan x \, dx$$

$$= \int (u^2 - 1) u^2 \cdot du = \int (u^4 - u^2) \, du$$

$$= \frac{u^5}{5} - \frac{u^3}{3} \Rightarrow \left[\frac{1}{5}(\sec x)^5 - \frac{1}{3}(\sec x)^3 \right]_0^{\pi/3}$$

$$\sec\frac{\pi}{3} = \frac{1}{\cos\frac{\pi}{3}} = \frac{1}{\frac{1}{2}} = 2 \qquad \sec 0 = \frac{1}{\cos 0} = 1$$

$$= \left(\frac{1}{5}(2^5) - \frac{1}{3}(2^3) \right) - \left(\frac{1}{5} - \frac{1}{3} \right)$$

$$= \frac{32}{5} - \frac{8}{3} - \frac{1}{5} + \frac{1}{3} = \frac{31}{5} - \frac{7}{3}$$

$$= \frac{93 - 35}{15} = \boxed{\frac{58}{15}}$$

2.5 Evaluate the integral

$$\int_{0}^{\pi/3} 15\sec^4(x)\tan^2(x)\,dx$$

(A) $42\sqrt{3}$ (C) $36\sqrt{3}$ (E) $45\sqrt{3}$ (G) $15\sqrt{3}$

(B) $\dfrac{4\pi}{3}$ (D) $27\sqrt{3}$ (F) $12\sqrt{3}$ (H) $30\sqrt{3}$

2.5 Evaluate the integral

$$\int_0^{\pi/3} 15\sec^4(x)\tan^2(x)\,dx$$

(A) $42\sqrt{3}$ (C) $36\sqrt{3}$ (E) $45\sqrt{3}$ (G) $15\sqrt{3}$

(B) $\dfrac{4\pi}{3}$ (D) $27\sqrt{3}$ (F) $12\sqrt{3}$ (H) $30\sqrt{3}$

Power of secx even:

- Factor out $\sec^2 x$

$$= \int_0^{\pi/3} 15\cdot\sec^2 x \cdot \tan^2 x \; \sec^2 x\, dx$$

- Transform remaining even powers of secx by $\sec^2 x = 1 + \tan^2 x$

$$= \int_0^{\pi/3} 15\cdot(1+\tan^2 x)\tan^2 x \; \sec^2 x\, dx$$

- Let $u = \tan x$
  $du = \sec^2 x\, dx$ $LL\ x=0\ \ u=0$
  $UL\ x=\frac{\pi}{3}\ \ u=\sqrt{3}$

$$= \int_0^{\sqrt{3}} 15\cdot(1+u^2)u^2\cdot du = 15\int_0^{\sqrt{3}}(u^2+u^4)du$$

$$= 15\cdot\left(\frac{u^3}{3}+\frac{u^5}{5}\right)\Big|_0^{\sqrt{3}} = \left(5u^3+3u^5\right)\Big|_0^{\sqrt{3}}$$

$$= 5(\sqrt{3})^3 + 3(\sqrt{3})^5 = \underbrace{5\cdot 3\sqrt{3}}_{15} + \underbrace{3\cdot 9\sqrt{3}}_{27}$$

$$= \boxed{42\sqrt{3}}$$

2.6 Evaluate the integral

$$\int_0^{\pi/12} \sin(3x)\sin x \, dx$$

(A) $\dfrac{3+\sqrt{3}}{12}$ (C) $\dfrac{4-\sqrt{3}}{3}$ (E) $\dfrac{4-\sqrt{2}}{8}$ (G) $\dfrac{4+\sqrt{2}}{8}$

(B) $\dfrac{2+\sqrt{2}}{4}$ (D) $\dfrac{3+\sqrt{2}}{12}$ (F) $\dfrac{2-\sqrt{3}}{16}$ (H) $\dfrac{2+\sqrt{3}}{16}$

2.6 Evaluate the integral

$$\int_0^{\pi/12} \sin(3x)\sin x \, dx$$

(A) $\dfrac{3+\sqrt{3}}{12}$ (C) $\dfrac{4-\sqrt{3}}{3}$ (E) $\dfrac{4-\sqrt{2}}{8}$ (G) $\dfrac{4+\sqrt{2}}{8}$

(B) $\dfrac{2+\sqrt{2}}{4}$ (D) $\dfrac{3+\sqrt{2}}{12}$ (F) $\dfrac{2-\sqrt{3}}{16}$ (H) $\dfrac{2+\sqrt{3}}{16}$

• **Use** $\sin(mx)\sin(nx) = \dfrac{1}{2}\left[\cos([m-n]x) - \cos([m+n]x)\right]$

with $m=3$ $n=1$

$$= \int_0^{\frac{\pi}{12}} \frac{1}{2}\left[\cos 2x - \cos 4x\right] dx$$

$$= \frac{1}{2}\left[\frac{1}{2}\sin 2x - \frac{1}{4}\sin 4x\right]_0^{\pi/12}$$

$$= \frac{1}{2}\left[\frac{1}{2}\sin\frac{\pi}{6} - \frac{1}{4}\sin\frac{\pi}{3}\right]$$

$$= \frac{1}{2}\left[\frac{1}{2}\cdot\frac{1}{2} - \frac{1}{4}\cdot\frac{\sqrt{3}}{2}\right]$$

$$= \frac{1}{2}\left[\frac{1}{4} - \frac{\sqrt{3}}{8}\right] = \frac{1}{2}\left[\frac{2-\sqrt{3}}{8}\right]$$

$$= \boxed{\frac{2-\sqrt{3}}{16}}$$

2.7 Evaluate the integral

$$\int_{1/2}^{1} \frac{\sqrt{1-x^2}}{x^2} \, dx$$

(A) 2   (C) 0   (E) $1-\dfrac{\pi}{4}$ (G) $\sqrt{3}-\dfrac{\pi}{3}$

(B) 1   (D) π (F) $\dfrac{\pi}{3}-2$

(H) $\dfrac{\pi}{2}$

2.7 Evaluate the integral

$$\int_{1/2}^{1} \frac{\sqrt{1-x^2}}{x^2}\, dx$$

(A) 2   (C) 0   (E) $1-\frac{\pi}{4}$ (G) $\sqrt{3}-\frac{\pi}{3}$

(B) 1   (D) π (F) $\frac{\pi}{3}-2$ (H) $\frac{\pi}{2}$

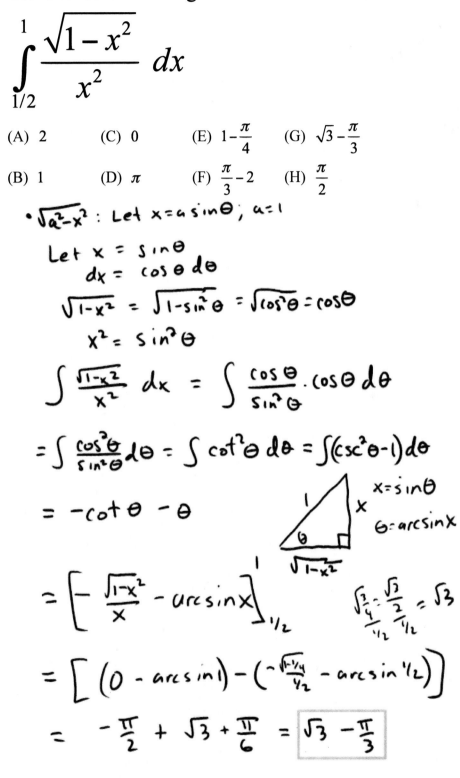

- $\sqrt{a^2-x^2}$: Let $x = a\sin\theta$; $a = 1$

  Let $x = \sin\theta$
  $dx = \cos\theta\, d\theta$
  $\sqrt{1-x^2} = \sqrt{1-\sin^2\theta} = \sqrt{\cos^2\theta} = \cos\theta$
  $x^2 = \sin^2\theta$

  $\int \frac{\sqrt{1-x^2}}{x^2}\, dx = \int \frac{\cos\theta}{\sin^2\theta}\cdot\cos\theta\, d\theta$

  $= \int \frac{\cos^2\theta}{\sin^2\theta}\, d\theta = \int \cot^2\theta\, d\theta = \int(\csc^2\theta - 1)\, d\theta$

  $= -\cot\theta - \theta$

  $x = \sin\theta$
  $\theta = \arcsin x$

  $= \left[-\frac{\sqrt{1-x^2}}{x} - \arcsin x \right]_{1/2}^{1}$

  $\frac{\sqrt{\frac{3}{4}}-\frac{\sqrt{3}}{2}}{\frac{1}{2}} \cdot \frac{1}{\frac{1}{2}} = \sqrt{3}$

  $= \left[(0 - \arcsin 1) - \left(-\frac{\sqrt{1-\frac{1}{4}}}{\frac{1}{2}} - \arcsin \frac{1}{2} \right) \right]$

  $= -\frac{\pi}{2} + \sqrt{3} + \frac{\pi}{6} = \boxed{\sqrt{3} - \frac{\pi}{3}}$

72

2.8 Evaluate the integral

$$\int_0^{5/2} \frac{12x^2}{\left(25 - x^2\right)^{3/2}}\, dx$$

(A) $2\sqrt{3}$　　(C) $\dfrac{\pi}{3}$　　(E) $\dfrac{\sqrt{3}}{2} + \dfrac{\pi}{4}$　　(G) $\sqrt{3} - \dfrac{\pi}{6}$

(B) 1　　(D) $\dfrac{\sqrt{3}}{3}$　　(F) $4\sqrt{3} - 2\pi$　　(H) $\dfrac{\pi}{6}$

2.8 Evaluate the integral

$$\int_0^{5/2} \frac{12x^2}{\left(25-x^2\right)^{3/2}}\, dx$$

(A) $2\sqrt{3}$ (C) $\dfrac{\pi}{3}$ (E) $\dfrac{\sqrt{3}}{2}+\dfrac{\pi}{4}$ (G) $\sqrt{3}-\dfrac{\pi}{6}$

(B) 1 (D) $\dfrac{\sqrt{3}}{3}$ (F) $4\sqrt{3}-2\pi$ (H) $\dfrac{\pi}{6}$

$\bullet\sqrt{a^2-x^2}$ Let $x=a\sin\theta$; $a=5$

Let $x=5\sin\theta$ $dx=5\cos\theta\, d\theta$

$(25-x^2)^{3/2}=(25-25\sin^2\theta)^{3/2}=(25(1-\sin^2\theta))^{3/2}$

$\qquad =(\sqrt{25\cos^2\theta})^3=(5\cos\theta)^3=5^3\cos^3\theta$

$12x^2=12(25\sin^2\theta)$

$\displaystyle\int\frac{12x^2}{(25-x^2)^{3/2}}dx=\int\frac{12\cdot 25\sin^2\theta}{5^3\cos^3\theta}5\cos\theta\, d\theta$

$=12\int\tan^2\theta\, d\theta = 12\int(\sec^2\theta-1)\, d\theta$

$=12\left(\tan\theta-\theta\right)$

$=12\left(\dfrac{x}{\sqrt{25-x^2}}-\arcsin\dfrac{x}{5}\right)\Bigg|_0^{5/2}$

$\sqrt{25-x^2}$

$\sin\theta=\dfrac{x}{5}$

$\theta=\arcsin(x/5)$

$=12\left(\left(\dfrac{5/2}{\sqrt{25-\frac{25}{4}}}-\arcsin\tfrac{1}{2}\right)-0\right)$ $\sqrt{25\cdot\tfrac{3}{4}}=\dfrac{5\sqrt{3}}{2}$

$=12\left(\dfrac{5/2}{\frac{5}{2}\sqrt{3}}-\dfrac{\pi}{6}\right)=12\left(\dfrac{\sqrt{3}}{3}-\dfrac{\pi}{6}\right)=\boxed{4\sqrt{3}-2\pi}$

74

2.9 Evaluate the integral

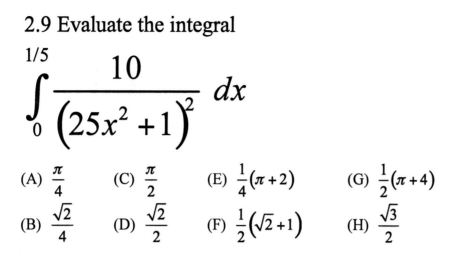

$$\int_0^{1/5} \frac{10}{\left(25x^2+1\right)^2}\, dx$$

(A) $\dfrac{\pi}{4}$　　(C) $\dfrac{\pi}{2}$　　(E) $\dfrac{1}{4}(\pi+2)$　　(G) $\dfrac{1}{2}(\pi+4)$

(B) $\dfrac{\sqrt{2}}{4}$　　(D) $\dfrac{\sqrt{2}}{2}$　　(F) $\dfrac{1}{2}(\sqrt{2}+1)$　　(H) $\dfrac{\sqrt{3}}{2}$

2.9 Evaluate the integral

$$\int_0^{1/5} \frac{10}{\left(25x^2 + 1\right)^2}\, dx$$

(A) $\dfrac{\pi}{4}$ (C) $\dfrac{\pi}{2}$ (E) $\dfrac{1}{4}(\pi + 2)$ (G) $\dfrac{1}{2}(\pi + 4)$

(B) $\dfrac{\sqrt{2}}{4}$ (D) $\dfrac{\sqrt{2}}{2}$ (F) $\dfrac{1}{2}(\sqrt{2} + 1)$ (H) $\dfrac{\sqrt{3}}{2}$

• $bx^2 + a^2 \Rightarrow$ factor out b

$$\left(25x^2 + 1\right)^2 = \left(25\left(x^2 + \tfrac{1}{25}\right)\right)^2 = 25^2\left(x^2 + \tfrac{1}{25}\right)^2$$

• $x^2 + a^2 \Rightarrow$ Let $x = a\tan\theta$; $a = \tfrac{1}{5}$

$x = \tfrac{1}{5}\tan\theta$ $\left(x^2 + \tfrac{1}{25}\right)^2 = \left(\tfrac{1}{25}(\tan^2\theta + 1)\right)^2$

$dx = \tfrac{1}{5}\sec^2\theta$ $= \left(\tfrac{1}{25}(\sec^2\theta)\right)^2$

$$\int \frac{10}{(25x^2+1)^2}\,dx = \int \frac{10 \cdot \tfrac{1}{5}\sec^2\theta}{25^2 \cdot \tfrac{1}{25^2}\sec^4\theta}\,d\theta$$

$$= 2\int \frac{1}{\sec^2\theta}\,d\theta = 2\int \cos^2\theta\,d\theta$$

$$= 2\int \tfrac{1}{2}(1 + \cos 2\theta)\,d\theta = \int (1 + \cos 2\theta)\,d\theta$$

$$= \theta + \tfrac{1}{2}\sin 2\theta = \theta + \tfrac{1}{2}\cdot 2\sin\theta\cos\theta$$

$$= \theta + \sin\theta\cos\theta$$

$$= \left[\arctan 5x + \frac{5x}{\sqrt{25x^2+1}} \cdot \frac{1}{\sqrt{25x^2+1}}\right]_0^{1/5}$$

$5x = \tan\theta$

$\theta = \arctan 5x$

$$= \left[\arctan 5x + \frac{5x}{25x^2+1}\right]_0^{1/5}$$

$$= \left(\arctan 1 + \frac{1}{1+1}\right) - (0 + 0)$$

$$= \tfrac{\pi}{4} + \tfrac{1}{2} = \boxed{\tfrac{1}{4}(\pi + 2)}$$

2.10 Solve the differential equation

$$\frac{dy}{dx} = \frac{1}{x^2\sqrt{x^2-9}} \quad \text{with } y(3) = 2.$$

2.10 Solve the differential equation

$$\frac{dy}{dx} = \frac{1}{x^2\sqrt{x^2-9}} \quad \text{with } y(3)=2.$$

$$\int dy = \int \frac{1}{x^2\sqrt{x^2-9}}\,dx$$

$$y = \int \frac{3\sec\theta\tan\theta\,d\theta}{9\sec^2\theta \cdot 3\tan\theta}$$

$$y = \frac{1}{9}\int \frac{1}{\sec\theta}\,d\theta$$

$$y = \frac{1}{9}\int \cos\theta\,d\theta$$

$$y = \frac{1}{9}\sin\theta$$

$$y = \frac{\sqrt{x^2-9}}{x} + C$$

$$y(3)=2$$

$$2 = \frac{\sqrt{9-9}}{3} + C \implies C = 2$$

$$\boxed{y = \frac{\sqrt{x^2-9}}{x} + 2}$$

• $\sqrt{x^2-a^2} \implies$ let $x = a\sec\theta$

$\qquad\qquad a = 3$

$x = 3\sec\theta$

$dx = 3\sec\theta\tan\theta\,d\theta$

$x^2 = 9\sec^2\theta$

$\sqrt{x^2-9} = \sqrt{9\sec^2\theta-9}$

$\qquad = \sqrt{9(\sec^2\theta-1)}$

$\qquad = 3\tan\theta$

$\frac{x}{3} = \sec\theta$

2.11 Find the volume of the solid generated by revolving the region bounded by

$$y = \frac{x^2}{\sqrt{9 - x^2}}, \ y = 0, \ \text{and} \ x = 2$$

about the y – axis.

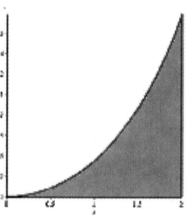

2.11 Find the volume of the solid generated by revolving the region bounded by

$$y = \frac{x^2}{\sqrt{9-x^2}}, \ \ y = 0, \ \text{and} \ x = 2$$

about the y – axis.

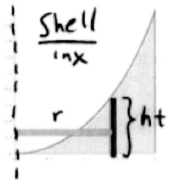

Shell
in x

r

}ht

$$V_{Shell} = 2\pi \int_0^2 x \cdot \frac{x^2}{\sqrt{9-x^2}} \, dx \qquad \begin{array}{l} radius = x \\ height = \dfrac{x^2}{\sqrt{9-x^2}} \end{array}$$

$$V = 2\pi \int_0^2 \frac{x^3}{\sqrt{9-x^2}} \, dx \qquad \sqrt{a^2-x^2} : Let \ x = a\sin\theta$$
$$\qquad\qquad\qquad\qquad x = 3\sin\theta$$
$$= 2\pi \int \frac{27\sin^3\theta \cdot 3\cos\theta}{3\cos\theta} \, d\theta \qquad dx = 3\cos\theta \, d\theta$$
$$\qquad\qquad\qquad\qquad x^3 = 27\sin^3\theta$$
$$= 54\pi \int \sin^3\theta \, d\theta \qquad \sqrt{9-x^2} = \sqrt{9(1-\sin^2\theta)}$$
$$= 54\pi \int \sin^2\theta \sin\theta \, d\theta \qquad \sqrt{9-x^2} = 3\cos\theta$$
$$= 54\pi \int (1-\cos^2\theta)\sin\theta \, d\theta \qquad \begin{array}{l} u = \cos\theta \\ du = -\sin\theta \, d\theta \end{array}$$
$$= 54\pi \left(\tfrac{1}{3}(\cos\theta)^3 - \cos\theta \right) \qquad \int (1-u^2)-1 \, du$$
$$\qquad\qquad\qquad\qquad \int (u^2-1) \, du$$
$$= 54\pi \left(\tfrac{1}{3}\left(\tfrac{\sqrt{9-x^2}}{3}\right)^3 - \tfrac{\sqrt{9-x^2}}{3} \right)\Big|^2 \qquad \tfrac{u^3}{3} - u$$
$$= 54\pi \left(\left[\tfrac{1}{3}\cdot\left(\tfrac{\sqrt5}{3}\right)^3 - \tfrac{\sqrt5}{3} \right] - \left[\tfrac{1}{3}\cdot 1 - 1 \right] \right)^0 \qquad \tfrac{x}{3} = \sin\theta$$
$$= 54\pi \left(\tfrac{\sqrt5}{3}\left(\tfrac{5}{27} - 1\right) + \tfrac{2}{3} \right)$$
$$= 54\pi \left(\tfrac{2}{3} - \tfrac{22}{27}\tfrac{\sqrt5}{3} \right) \qquad \cos\theta \ \tfrac{\sqrt{9-x^2}}{3}$$
$$= \tfrac{54\pi \cdot 2}{3} - \tfrac{54\pi \cdot 22\sqrt5}{81}$$
$$= \boxed{36\pi - \frac{44\sqrt5}{3}}$$

2.12 Evaluate the integral

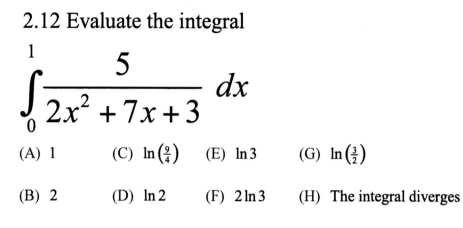

$$\int_0^1 \frac{5}{2x^2 + 7x + 3}\, dx$$

(A) 1   (C) $\ln\left(\frac{9}{4}\right)$ (E) $\ln 3$ (G) $\ln\left(\frac{3}{2}\right)$

(B) 2   (D) $\ln 2$ (F) $2\ln 3$ (H) The integral diverges

2.12 Evaluate the integral

$$\int_0^1 \frac{5}{2x^2 + 7x + 3}\, dx$$

(A) 1   (C) $\ln\left(\frac{9}{4}\right)$ (E) $\ln 3$ (G) $\ln\left(\frac{3}{2}\right)$

(B) 2   (D) $\ln 2$ (F) $2\ln 3$ (H) The integral diverges

$$2x^2 + 7x + 3 = (2x+1)(x+3)$$

$$\int_0^1 \frac{5\, dx}{(2x+1)(x+3)} = \int_0^1 \left(\frac{A}{2x+1} + \frac{B}{x+3}\right) dx$$

$$A(x+3) + B(2x+1) = 5$$

let
$x = -3$ $B(-5) = 5$ $B = -1$

let
$x = \frac{-1}{2}$ $A\left(\frac{5}{2}\right) = 5$ $A = 2$

$$= \int_0^1 \left(\frac{2}{2x+1} - \frac{1}{x+3}\right) dx$$

$$= \left[\ln|2x+1| - \ln|x+3|\right]_0^1$$

$$= (\ln 3 - \ln 4) - (\ln 1 - \ln 3)$$

$$= 2\ln 3 - \ln 4$$

$$= \ln 3^2 - \ln 4 = \boxed{\ln\left(\frac{9}{4}\right)}$$

82

2.13 Evaluate the integral

$$\int_{0}^{2} \frac{5x^2 - 2x + 2}{x^3 + 1} \, dx$$

Hint: $a^3 + b^3 = (a+b)(a^2 - ab + b^2)$

(A) $2\ln 6$ (C) $3\ln 6$ (E) $4\ln 3$ (G) $4\ln 2$

(B) $6\ln 3$ (D) $3\ln 2$ (F) $2\ln 3$ (H) $6\ln 2$

2.13 Evaluate the integral

$$\int_0^2 \frac{5x^2 - 2x + 2}{x^3 + 1} \, dx$$

Hint: $a^3 + b^3 = (a+b)(a^2 - ab + b^2)$

(A) $2\ln 6$ (C) $3\ln 6$ (E) $4\ln 3$ (G) $4\ln 2$

(B) $6\ln 3$ (D) $3\ln 2$ (F) $2\ln 3$ (H) $6\ln 2$

$$x^3 + 1 = (x+1)(x^2 - x + 1)$$

$$\int_0^2 \frac{5x^2 - 2x + 2}{x^3 + 1}\, dx = \int_0^2 \left(\frac{A}{x+1} + \frac{Bx+C}{x^2 - x + 1}\right) dx$$

$$A(x^2 - x + 1) + (Bx + C)(x + 1) = 5x^2 - 2x + 2$$

$$\text{let} \atop x = -1 \qquad A(1 + 1 + 1) = 5 + 2 + 2$$
$$3A = 9 \qquad A = 3$$

$$\text{let} \atop x = 0 \qquad A + C = 2$$
$$3 + C = 2 \qquad C = -1$$

$$\text{let} \atop x = 1 \qquad A + 2(B + C) = 5 - 2 + 2$$
$$3 + 2(B - 1) = 5$$
$$2(B - 1) = 2$$
$$B - 1 = 1$$
$$B = 2$$

$$= \int_0^2 \left(\frac{3}{x+1} + \frac{2x - 1}{x^2 - x + 1}\right) dx \qquad \begin{array}{l} u = x^2 - x + 1 \\ du = (2x - 1)dx \end{array}$$

$$= \left[3\ln|x+1| + \ln|x^2 - x + 1|\right]_0^2$$

$$= (3\ln 3 + \ln 3) - (3\ln 1 + \ln 1)$$

$$= 4\ln 3$$

2.14 Evaluate the integral

$$\int_{\sqrt{3}}^{3} \frac{3x^2 + 3x + 9}{x^3 + 9x}\, dx$$

(A) $\dfrac{\pi}{3} + \ln\left(\dfrac{2}{3}\right)$ (C) $\dfrac{\pi}{6} + \ln\left(\dfrac{3}{2}\right)$ (E) $\dfrac{\pi}{12} + \ln\left(\dfrac{4}{3}\right)$ (G) $\dfrac{\pi}{15} + \ln 2$

(B) $\dfrac{\pi}{12} + \ln\left(\dfrac{3\sqrt{3}}{2}\right)$ (D) $\ln(3) - \dfrac{\pi}{4}$ (F) $\ln\left(\dfrac{\sqrt{3}}{2}\right) + \dfrac{\pi}{6}$ (H) $\dfrac{\pi}{5}\ln 3$

2.14 Evaluate the integral

$$\int_{\sqrt{3}}^{3} \frac{3x^2 + 3x + 9}{x^3 + 9x} \, dx$$

(A) $\dfrac{\pi}{3} + \ln\left(\dfrac{2}{3}\right)$ (C) $\dfrac{\pi}{6} + \ln\left(\dfrac{3}{2}\right)$ (E) $\dfrac{\pi}{12} + \ln\left(\dfrac{4}{3}\right)$ (G) $\dfrac{\pi}{15} + \ln 2$

(B) $\dfrac{\pi}{12} + \ln\left(\dfrac{3\sqrt{3}}{2}\right)$ (D) $\ln(3) - \dfrac{\pi}{4}$ (F) $\ln\left(\dfrac{\sqrt{3}}{2}\right) + \dfrac{\pi}{6}$ (H) $\dfrac{\pi}{5}\ln 3$

$x^3 + 9x = x(x^2 + 9)$ irreducible quadratic

$$\int_{\sqrt{3}}^{3} \frac{3x^2 + 3x + 9}{x^3 + 9x} dx = \int_{\sqrt{3}}^{3} \left(\frac{A}{x} + \frac{Bx + C}{x^2 + 9}\right) dx$$

$A(x^2 + 9) + (Bx + C)\cdot x = 3x^2 + 3x + 9$

let $x = 0$ $9A = 9$ $A = 1$

let $x = 1$ $10A + (B + C) = 3 + 3 + 9$

$10 + B + C = 15$

$B + C = 5$

let $x = -1$ $10A + (-B + C)(-1) = 3 - 3 + 9$

$10 + B - C = 9$

$B - C = -1$

$\begin{array}{l} B + C = 5 \\ B - C = -1 \\ \hline 2B = 4 \\ B = 2 \end{array}$ $\begin{array}{l} 2 + C = 5 \\ C = 3 \end{array}$

$$\int_{\sqrt{3}}^{3} \left(\frac{1}{x} + \frac{2x + 3}{x^2 + 9}\right) dx = \int_{\sqrt{3}}^{3}\left(\frac{1}{x} + \frac{2x}{x^2 + 9} + \frac{3}{x^2 + 9}\right) dx$$

$$= \left[\ln|x| + \ln|x^2 + 9| + 3 \cdot \frac{1}{3}\arctan\left(\frac{x}{3}\right)\right]_{\sqrt{3}}^{3}$$

$$= (\ln 3 + \ln 18 + \arctan 1) - \left(\ln\sqrt{3} + \ln 12 + \arctan\frac{\sqrt{3}}{3}\right)$$

$$= \ln 3 + \ln 18 + \frac{\pi}{4} - \ln\sqrt{3} - \ln 12 - \frac{\pi}{6}$$

$$= \ln\left(\frac{3 \cdot 18}{\sqrt{3} \cdot 12}\right) + \frac{3\pi - 2\pi}{12} = \ln\left(\frac{9}{2\sqrt{3}}\right) + \frac{\pi}{12}$$

$$= \ln\left(\frac{9 \cdot \sqrt{3}}{2 \cdot \sqrt{3} \cdot \sqrt{3}}\right) + \frac{\pi}{12} = \boxed{\ln\left(\frac{3\sqrt{3}}{2}\right) + \frac{\pi}{12}}$$

2.15 Evaluate the integral

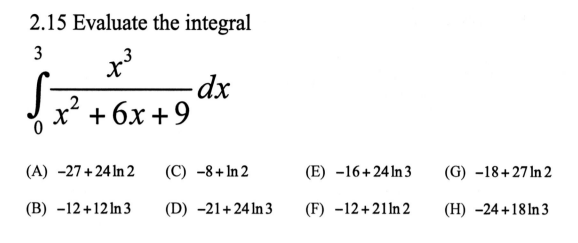

$$\int_{0}^{3} \frac{x^3}{x^2 + 6x + 9}\, dx$$

(A) $-27 + 24\ln 2$ (C) $-8 + \ln 2$ (E) $-16 + 24\ln 3$ (G) $-18 + 27\ln 2$

(B) $-12 + 12\ln 3$ (D) $-21 + 24\ln 3$ (F) $-12 + 21\ln 2$ (H) $-24 + 18\ln 3$

2.15 Evaluate the integral

$$\int_0^3 \frac{x^3}{x^2 + 6x + 9}\, dx$$

(A) $-27 + 24\ln 2$ (C) $-8 + \ln 2$ (E) $-16 + 24\ln 3$ (G) $-18 + 27\ln 2$

(B) $-12 + 12\ln 3$ (D) $-21 + 24\ln 3$ (F) $-12 + 21\ln 2$ (H) $-24 + 18\ln 3$

Deg. den < Deg. num ⟹ Long Divide

$$x^2 + 6x + 9 \,\overline{\big)\, x^3}$$
quotient: $x - 6$

$$-(x^3 + 6x^2 + 9x)$$
$$-6x^2 - 9x$$
$$-(-6x^2 - 36x - 54)$$
$$27x + 54$$

$$= \int_0^3 \left(x - 6 + \frac{27x + 54}{x^2 + 6x + 9}\right) dx$$

$(x+3)(x+3) = (x+3)^2$

$$= \int_0^3 \left(x - 6 + \frac{A}{x+3} + \frac{B}{(x+3)^2}\right) dx$$

$A(x+3) + B = 27x + 54$

let $x = -3$ $B = -81 + 54 = -27$

let $x = 0$ $3A + B = 54$
$$3A - 27 = 54$$
$$3A = 81$$
$$A = 27$$

$$= \int_0^3 \left[x - 6 + 27\left(\frac{1}{x+3} + \frac{-1}{(x+3)^2}\right)\right] dx$$

$$= \left(\frac{x^2}{2} - 6x + 27\left[\ln|x+3| + \frac{1}{x+3}\right]\right)\Big|_0^3$$

$$= \left(\frac{9}{2} - 18 + 27\left[\ln 6 + \frac{1}{6}\right]\right) - \left(0 - 0 + 27\left(\ln 3 + \frac{1}{3}\right)\right)$$

$$= \frac{9}{2} - 18 + 27\ln 6 + \frac{27}{6} - 27\ln 3 - 9$$

$$= 27\left(\ln 6 - \ln 3\right) + \frac{9}{2} + \frac{9}{2} - 18 - 9$$

$$= 27\ln\left(\frac{6}{3}\right) + 9 - 18 - 9 = \boxed{27\ln 2 - 18}$$

88

2.16 Consider the probability density function whose graph $f(x)$ is displayed below.

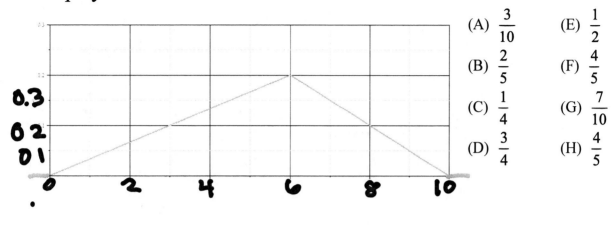

(A) $\dfrac{3}{10}$ (E) $\dfrac{1}{2}$

(B) $\dfrac{2}{5}$ (F) $\dfrac{4}{5}$

(C) $\dfrac{1}{4}$ (G) $\dfrac{7}{10}$

(D) $\dfrac{3}{4}$ (H) $\dfrac{4}{5}$

$f(x)=0$ for $x<0$ and $x>10$. Find the probability that $3 \le x \le 8$.

2.16 Consider the probability density function whose graph $f(x)$ is displayed below.

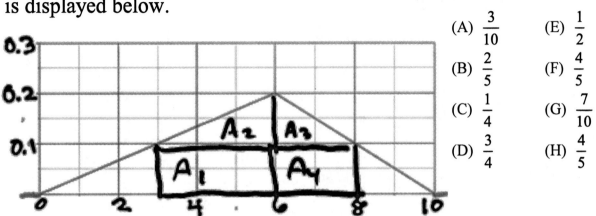

(A) $\dfrac{3}{10}$ (E) $\dfrac{1}{2}$

(B) $\dfrac{2}{5}$ (F) $\dfrac{4}{5}$

(C) $\dfrac{1}{4}$ (G) $\dfrac{7}{10}$

(D) $\dfrac{3}{4}$ (H) $\dfrac{4}{5}$

$f(x) = 0$ for $x < 0$ and $x > 10$. Find the probability that $3 \le x \le 8$.

$$P(3 \le x \le 8) = A_1 + A_2 + A_3 + A_4$$

$$= 0.1(3) + \tfrac{1}{2}(0.1)(3) + \tfrac{1}{2}(0.1)(2) + 0.1(2)$$

$$= 0.3 + \tfrac{1}{2}(0.3) + \tfrac{1}{2}(0.2) + 0.2$$

$$= 0.3 + 0.15 + 0.1 + 0.2$$

$$= \underbrace{0.45} + \underbrace{0.3} = 0.75$$

$$= \boxed{\dfrac{3}{4}}$$

2.17 $f(x)$ below is a probability density function. Find its mean.

$$f(x) = \begin{cases} 16xe^{-4x} & \text{if } x \geq 0 \\ 0 & x < 0 \end{cases}$$

(A) $\dfrac{1}{2}$ (E) $\dfrac{2}{3}$

(B) $\dfrac{1}{3}$ (F) $\dfrac{3}{4}$

(C) $\dfrac{1}{4}$ (G) 1

(D) $\dfrac{1}{8}$ (H) $\dfrac{3}{2}$

2.17 $f(x)$ below is a probability density function. Find its mean.

$$f(x) = \begin{cases} 16xe^{-4x} & \text{if } x \geq 0 \\ 0 & x < 0 \end{cases}$$

(A) $\dfrac{1}{2}$ (E) $\dfrac{2}{3}$

(B) $\dfrac{1}{3}$ (F) $\dfrac{3}{4}$

(C) $\dfrac{1}{4}$ (G) 1

(D) $\dfrac{1}{8}$ (H) $\dfrac{3}{2}$

$$\mu = \int_{-\infty}^{\infty} x \cdot f(x)dx = \int_0^{\infty} 16x^2 e^{-4x} dx$$

Since $f = 0$ for $x < 0$

Use integration by parts shortcut

$$\frac{D}{16x^2} \qquad \frac{I}{e^{-4x}}$$

$$32x \qquad -\tfrac{1}{4}e^{-4x}$$

$$32 \qquad \tfrac{1}{16}e^{-4x}$$

$$0 \qquad -\tfrac{1}{64}e^{-4x}$$

$$= \lim_{b\to\infty}\left[-4x^2 e^{-4x} - 2xe^{-4x} - \tfrac{1}{2}e^{-4x}\right]_0^b$$

$$= \lim_{b\to\infty}\left[\frac{-4x^2 - 2x - \tfrac{1}{2}}{e^{4x}}\right]_0^b$$

$$= \lim_{b\to\infty} \frac{-4b^2 - 2b - \tfrac{1}{2}}{e^{4b}} - \frac{-\tfrac{1}{2}}{1}$$

$$= \underbrace{0}_{} + \tfrac{1}{2} = \boxed{\tfrac{1}{2}}$$

$$\lim_{b\to\infty}\frac{-4b^2 - 2b - \tfrac{1}{2}}{e^{4b}} \overset{"\frac{-\infty}{\infty}"}{=} \overset{L'Hop}{=} \lim_{b\to\infty}\frac{-8b-2}{4e^{4b}} \overset{"\frac{-\infty}{\infty}"}{=}$$

$$\overset{L'Hop}{=} \lim_{b\to\infty}\frac{-8}{16e^{4b}} = 0$$

2.18 Find the value of k so that the function below is a probability density function.

$$f(x) = \begin{cases} kx^2(3-x) & 0 \le x \le 3 \\ 0 & x < 0 \text{ or } x > 3 \end{cases}$$

(A) $\dfrac{7}{3}$ (E) $\dfrac{2}{3}$

(B) $\dfrac{1}{3}$ (F) $\dfrac{2}{9}$

(C) $\dfrac{5}{9}$ (G) $\dfrac{4}{27}$

(D) $\dfrac{4}{3}$ (H) $\dfrac{11}{27}$

2.18 Find the value of k so that the function below is a probability density function.

$$f(x) = \begin{cases} kx^2(3-x) & 0 \le x \le 3 \\ 0 & x < 0 \text{ or } x > 3 \end{cases}$$

(A) $\dfrac{7}{3}$ (E) $\dfrac{2}{3}$

(B) $\dfrac{1}{3}$ (F) $\dfrac{2}{9}$

(C) $\dfrac{5}{9}$ (G) $\dfrac{4}{27}$

(D) $\dfrac{4}{3}$ (H) $\dfrac{11}{27}$

For a function to be a prob. dens. function,

① $f(x) \ge 0$ for all x

✓ for $x < 0$ or $x > 3$, $f = 0$

for $0 \le x \le 3$

$f = K x^2 (3-X) \Rightarrow K$ must be > 0
       +   +

② $\displaystyle\int_{-\infty}^{\infty} f(x)\,dx = 1$ since $f = 0$ for $x < 0$ and $x > 3$,

$\Rightarrow \displaystyle\int_{0}^{3} Kx^2(3-x)\,dx = 1$ Factor out K and simplify

$K\displaystyle\int_{0}^{3}(3x^2-x^3)\,dx = 1$ Integrate

$K \cdot \left[x^3 - \dfrac{x^4}{4} \right]_{0}^{3} = 1 \Rightarrow K\left[\left(3^3 - \dfrac{3^4}{4}\right) - 0\right] = 1$ Factor out 3^3

$K\left[3^3\left(1 - \dfrac{3}{4}\right)\right] = 1$

$27K \cdot \dfrac{1}{4} = 1$ mult. by $\dfrac{4}{27}$

$\therefore \boxed{K = \dfrac{4}{27}}$

94

2.19 $f(x)$ below is a probability density function. Find its median.

$$f(x) = \begin{cases} \dfrac{2}{x^3} & \text{if } x \geq 1 \\ 0 & x < 1 \end{cases}$$

(A) 2 (E) 3

(B) $\sqrt{2}$ (F) $\sqrt{3}$

(C) 4 (G) 1

(D) $\sqrt[3]{3}$ (H) $\sqrt[3]{2}$

2.19 $f(x)$ below is a probability density function. Find its median.

$$f(x) = \begin{cases} \dfrac{2}{x^3} & \text{if } x \geq 1 \\[2mm] 0 & x < 1 \end{cases}$$

(A) 2   (E) 3

(B) $\sqrt{2}$ (F) $\sqrt{3}$

(C) 4   (G) 1

(D) $\sqrt[3]{3}$ (H) $\sqrt[3]{2}$

Median m is found by solving

$$\int_m^\infty f(x)\,dx = \frac{1}{2} \quad \text{or} \quad \int_{-\infty}^m f(x)\,dx = \frac{1}{2}$$

$f = 0$ for $x < 1$ and $f = \dfrac{2}{x^3}$ for $x \geq 1$

So this makes the second integral become

$$\int_1^m \frac{2}{x^3}\,dx = \frac{1}{2} \quad \Rightarrow \quad 2\int_1^m x^{-3}\,dx = \frac{1}{2}$$

$$2\left[\frac{x^{-2}}{-2}\right]_1^m = \frac{1}{2} \quad \Rightarrow \quad \left[\frac{-1}{x^2}\right]_1^m = \frac{1}{2}$$

$$\frac{-1}{m^2} - {}^-1 = \frac{1}{2} \quad \Rightarrow \quad \frac{-1}{m^2} + 1 = \frac{1}{2}$$

$$\frac{-1}{m^2} = \frac{-1}{2} \quad \text{or} \quad m^2 = 2 \quad \therefore \boxed{m = \sqrt{2}}$$

2.20 Evaluate the integral

$$\int_{-14}^{2} \frac{dx}{(2-x)^{3/4}}$$

(A) 12   (C) 3   (E) 4   (G) 8

(B) 2   (D) 16   (F) 15   (H) The integral diverges.

2.20 Evaluate the integral

$$\int_{-14}^{2} \frac{dx}{(2-x)^{3/4}}$$

(A) 12   (C) 3   (E) 4   (G) 8

(B) 2   (D) 16   (F) 15   (H) The integral diverges.

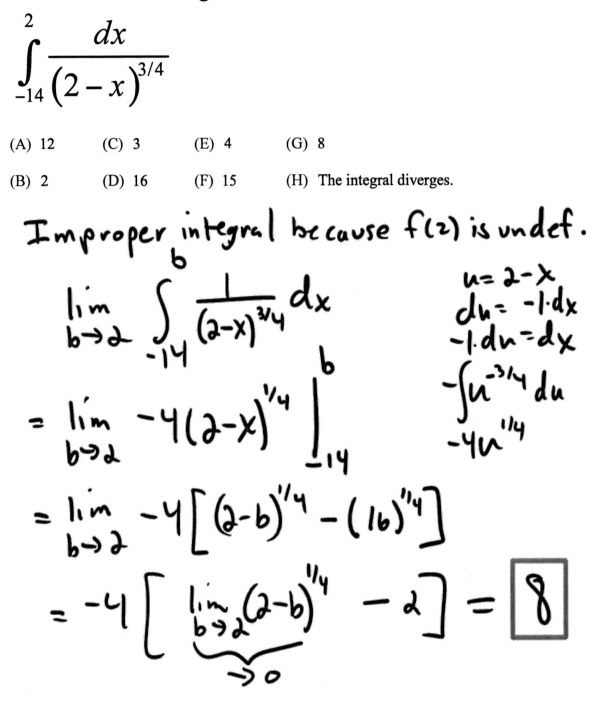

Improper integral because $f(2)$ is undef.

$$\lim_{b \to 2} \int_{-14}^{b} \frac{1}{(2-x)^{3/4}} dx$$

$u = 2-x$
$du = -1 \cdot dx$
$-1 \cdot du = dx$

$$-\int u^{-3/4} du$$

$$= \lim_{b \to 2} -4(2-x)^{1/4} \Big|_{-14}^{b}$$

$-4u^{1/4}$

$$= \lim_{b \to 2} -4 \left[(2-b)^{1/4} - (16)^{1/4} \right]$$

$$= -4 \left[\underbrace{\lim_{b \to 2} (2-b)^{1/4}}_{\to 0} - 2 \right] = \boxed{8}$$

2.21 Evaluate the integral

$$\int_{1}^{\infty} \frac{\ln x}{x^{4/3}}\, dx$$

(A) 4

(B) $\dfrac{4}{9}$

(C) 2

(D) $\dfrac{1}{2}$

(E) $\dfrac{4}{3}$

(F) 9

(G) 1

(H) The integral diverges

2.21 Evaluate the integral

$$\int_1^\infty \frac{\ln x}{x^{4/3}}\, dx$$

(A) 4 (E) $\dfrac{4}{3}$

(B) $\dfrac{4}{9}$ (F) 9

(C) 2 (G) 1

(D) $\dfrac{1}{2}$ (H) The integral diverges

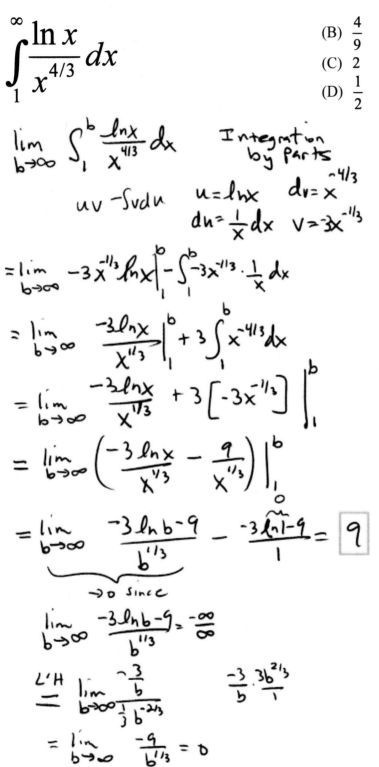

$$\lim_{b\to\infty} \int_1^b \frac{\ln x}{x^{4/3}}\, dx \qquad \text{Integration by parts}$$

$$uv - \int v\, du \qquad u = \ln x \qquad dv = x^{-4/3}$$
$$du = \frac{1}{x}\, dx \qquad v = -3x^{-1/3}$$

$$= \lim_{b\to\infty} \left. -3x^{-1/3} \ln x \right|_1^b - \int_1^b -3x^{-1/3}\cdot \frac{1}{x}\, dx$$

$$= \lim_{b\to\infty} \left. \frac{-3\ln x}{x^{1/3}}\right|_1^b + 3\int_1^b x^{-4/3}\, dx$$

$$= \lim_{b\to\infty} \frac{-3\ln x}{x^{1/3}} + 3\left[-3x^{-1/3}\right]\Big|_1^b$$

$$= \lim_{b\to\infty} \left(\frac{-3\ln x}{x^{1/3}} - \frac{9}{x^{1/3}}\right)\Big|_1^b$$

$$= \lim_{b\to\infty} \frac{-3\ln b - 9}{b^{1/3}} - \frac{-3\ln 1 - 9}{1} = \boxed{9}$$

$$\underbrace{\qquad\qquad}_{\to 0 \text{ since}}$$

$$\lim_{b\to\infty} \frac{-3\ln b - 9}{b^{1/3}} = \frac{-\infty}{\infty}$$

$$\overset{L'H}{=} \lim_{b\to\infty} \frac{-\frac{3}{b}}{\frac{1}{3}b^{-2/3}} \qquad \frac{-3}{b}\cdot\frac{3b^{2/3}}{1}$$

$$= \lim_{b\to\infty} \frac{-9}{b^{1/3}} = 0$$

2.22 Find the volume of the solid generated by revolving the region in the first quadrant under the curve $y = \dfrac{10}{x^2}$ bounded on the left by $x = 1,$ unbounded on the right, rotated about the x – axis.

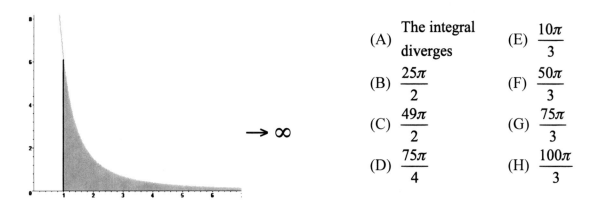

(A) The integral diverges

(B) $\dfrac{25\pi}{2}$

(C) $\dfrac{49\pi}{2}$

(D) $\dfrac{75\pi}{4}$

(E) $\dfrac{10\pi}{3}$

(F) $\dfrac{50\pi}{3}$

(G) $\dfrac{75\pi}{3}$

(H) $\dfrac{100\pi}{3}$

2.22 Find the volume of the solid generated by revolving the region in the first quadrant under the curve $y = \dfrac{10}{x^2}$ bounded on the left by $x = 1$, unbounded on the right, rotated about the x – axis.

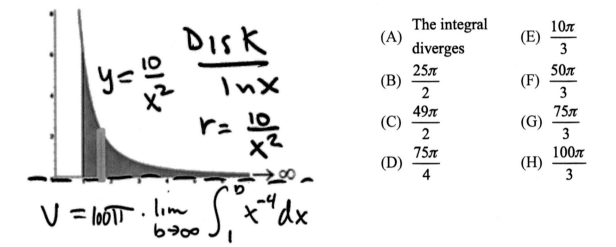

(A) The integral diverges

(B) $\dfrac{25\pi}{2}$

(C) $\dfrac{49\pi}{2}$

(D) $\dfrac{75\pi}{4}$

(E) $\dfrac{10\pi}{3}$

(F) $\dfrac{50\pi}{3}$

(G) $\dfrac{75\pi}{3}$

(H) $\dfrac{100\pi}{3}$

DISK

$\dfrac{}{\ln x}$

$r = \dfrac{10}{x^2}$

$V = 100\pi \cdot \lim_{b \to \infty} \int_1^b x^{-4}\,dx$

$V = 100\pi \lim_{b \to \infty} \left[\dfrac{x^{-3}}{-3} \right]_1^b$

$V = 100\pi \lim_{b \to \infty} \left[\dfrac{-1}{3x^3} \right]_1^b \quad \leftarrow \quad \dfrac{-1}{3}\left[\dfrac{1}{x^3} \right]$

$V = 100\pi \left[\dfrac{-1}{3}\left(\left(\lim_{b \to \infty} \dfrac{1}{b^3} \right) - 1 \right) \right]$

$\to 0$

$V = 100\pi \left(\dfrac{-1}{3} \cdot -1 \right)$

$\boxed{V = \dfrac{100\pi}{3} \text{ units}^2}$

102

2.23 Find the area of the region enclosed by the graphs of
$y = \dfrac{1}{x+1}$ and $y = \dfrac{1}{x+3}$ on the interval $[0, \infty)$.

(A) $\ln 3$ (E) $\sqrt{3}$

(B) $\ln 4$ (F) $\dfrac{1}{2}$

(C) 0 (G) 1

(D) 2 (H) ∞

2.23 Find the area of the region enclosed by the graphs of

$y = \dfrac{1}{x+1}$ and $y = \dfrac{1}{x+3}$ on the interval $[0,\infty)$.

(A) ln 3   (E) $\sqrt{3}$

(B) ln 4   (F) $\dfrac{1}{2}$

(C) 0   (G) 1

(D) 2   (H) ∞

$y = \dfrac{1}{x+1}$

$y = \dfrac{1}{x+3}$

$\to \infty$

@ $x=0$ $y = \dfrac{1}{x+1}$ will be 1 while $y = \dfrac{1}{x+3}$ will be $\dfrac{1}{3}$

$\text{Area} = \displaystyle\int_0^\infty \left(\dfrac{1}{x+1} - \dfrac{1}{x+3}\right)dx$

$= \displaystyle\lim_{b\to\infty}\left(\ln|x+1| - \ln|x+3|\right)\Big|_0^b$

$= \displaystyle\lim_{b\to\infty}\left(\ln(b+1) - \ln(b+3)\right) - \underbrace{\left(\ln 1 - \ln 3\right)}_{0}$

$= \displaystyle\lim_{b\to\infty}\ln\left(\dfrac{b+1}{b+3}\right) + \ln 3$

$= \ln\left(\underbrace{\displaystyle\lim_{b\to\infty}\dfrac{b+1}{b+3}}_{\to 1}\right) + \ln 3 = \boxed{\ln 3}$

$\ln 1 = 0$

2.24 Determine whether the integral converges or diverges by using one of the comparison theorems.

I. $\displaystyle\int_{4}^{\infty}\frac{2+\cos x}{\sqrt[3]{x}}\,dx$ II. $\displaystyle\int_{2}^{\infty}\frac{x}{\sqrt{x^5+4}}\,dx$

(A) Both (I) and (II) converge.   (C) (I) converges and (II) diverges.

(B) Both (I) and (II) diverge.   (D) (I) diverges and (II) converges.

2.24 Determine whether the integral converges or diverges by using one of the comparison theorems.

I. $\displaystyle\int_4^{\infty}\frac{2+\cos x}{\sqrt[3]{x}}\,dx$

II. $\displaystyle\int_2^{\infty}\frac{x}{\sqrt{x^5+4}}\,dx$

(A) Both (I) and (II) converge.

(C) (I) converges and (II) diverges.

(B) Both (I) and (II) diverge.

(D) (I) diverges and (II) converges.

I. Compare to $\displaystyle\int_4^{\infty}\frac{1}{x^{1/3}}dx = \lim_{b\to\infty}\int_4^b x^{-1/3}dx$

$\text{Diverges} \nearrow$

$\qquad\qquad = \lim_{b\to\infty}\frac{3}{2}x^{2/3}\Big|_4^b = \lim_{b\to\infty}\frac{3}{2}\left(b^{2/3}-4^{2/3}\right) = \infty$

$\dfrac{1}{x^{1/3}} \le \dfrac{2+\cos x}{x^{1/3}} \qquad$ so $\qquad \displaystyle\int_4^{\infty}\frac{1}{x^{1/3}}dx \le \int_4^{\infty}\frac{2+\cos x}{x^{1/3}}dx$

$\therefore$ By the Direct Comparison Test,

$\displaystyle\int_4^{\infty}\frac{2+\cos x}{x^{1/3}}dx$ also $\boxed{\text{Diverges}}$

II. Compare to $\displaystyle\int_2^{\infty}\frac{x}{x^{5/2}}dx = \int_2^{\infty}x^{-3/2}dx$

$\qquad\qquad = \lim_{b\to\infty}2x^{-1/2}\Big|_2^b = \lim_{b\to\infty}\frac{2}{\sqrt{x}}\Big|_2^b$

$\qquad\qquad = \lim_{b\to\infty}\frac{2}{\sqrt{b}}-\frac{2}{\sqrt{2}} = \frac{-2}{\sqrt{2}} \quad$ Converges

$\dfrac{x}{\sqrt{x^5+4}} \le \dfrac{x}{\sqrt{x^5}} \qquad$ so $\qquad \displaystyle\int_2^{\infty}\frac{x}{\sqrt{x^5+4}}dx \le \int_2^{\infty}x^{-3/2}dx$

larger denom $\Rightarrow$ smaller fraction

$\therefore$ By the Direct Comparison Test,

$\displaystyle\int_2^{\infty}\frac{x}{\sqrt{x^5+4}}dx$ also $\boxed{\text{Converges}}$

2.25 Determine whether the integral converges or diverges by using one of the comparison theorems.

I. $\displaystyle\int_{5}^{\infty} \frac{3}{\sqrt{e^x - x}}\,dx$ II. $\displaystyle\int_{1}^{\infty} \frac{\sqrt{x^7 - 5}}{x^4}\,dx$

(A) Both (I) and (II) converge.   (C) (I) converges and (II) diverges.

(B) Both (I) and (II) diverge.   (D) (I) diverges and (II) converges.

2.25 Determine whether the integral converges or diverges by using one of the comparison theorems.

I. $\displaystyle\int_{5}^{\infty}\frac{3}{\sqrt{e^x-x}}\,dx$
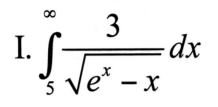

II. $\displaystyle\int_{1}^{\infty}\frac{\sqrt{x^7-5}}{x^4}\,dx$
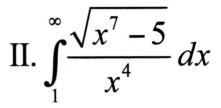

(A) Both (I) and (II) converge.

(C) (I) converges and (II) diverges.

(B) Both (I) and (II) diverge.

(D) (I) diverges and (II) converges.

I. compare to $\displaystyle\int_{5}^{\infty}\frac{3}{\sqrt{e^x}}\,dx=\int_{5}^{\infty}3\cdot e^{-x/2}\,dx$

$=\displaystyle\lim_{b\to\infty}6e^{-x/2}\Big|_{5}^{b}$

$=\displaystyle\lim_{b\to\infty}6\left[\frac{1}{e^{b/2}}-\frac{1}{e^{5/2}}\right]=\frac{6}{e^{5/2}}$ Converges

$\dfrac{3}{\sqrt{e^x}}<\dfrac{3}{\sqrt{e^x-x}}$ ✓ smaller denom ⇒ larger ⇒ wrong Direction for Direct Comp.

Limit Comparison

$\displaystyle\lim_{x\to\infty}\frac{\frac{3}{\sqrt{e^x-x}}}{\frac{3}{\sqrt{e^x}}}=\lim_{x\to\infty}\frac{3}{\sqrt{e^x-x}}\cdot\frac{\sqrt{e^x}}{3}=\lim_{x\to\infty}\sqrt{\frac{e^x}{e^x-x}}=1$

So they behave alike

∴ By the Limit Comparison Theorem,

$\displaystyle\int_{5}^{\infty}\frac{3}{\sqrt{e^x-x}}\,dx$ also $\boxed{\text{Converges}}$

II. Compare to $\displaystyle\int_{1}^{\infty}\frac{\sqrt{x^7}}{x^4}\,dx=\int_{1}^{\infty}\frac{x^{7/2}}{x^4}\,dx=\int_{1}^{\infty}x^{-1/2}\,dx$

$=\displaystyle\lim_{b\to\infty}2\sqrt{x}\Big|_{1}^{b}=\lim_{b\to\infty}2\sqrt{b}-2=\infty$

$\dfrac{\sqrt{x^7-5}}{x^4}<\dfrac{\sqrt{x^7}}{x^4}$ ⇒ wrong Direction for Direct Comp Thm.

smaller numer. < same denom

So smaller

Limit Comp. Thm. $\displaystyle\lim_{b\to\infty}\frac{\frac{\sqrt{x^7-5}}{x^4}}{\frac{\sqrt{x^7}}{x^4}}=\lim_{b\to\infty}\frac{\sqrt{x^7-5}}{x^4}\cdot\frac{x^4}{\sqrt{x^7}}$

$=\displaystyle\lim_{b\to\infty}\frac{\sqrt{x^7-5}}{\sqrt{x^7}}=1$ so they behave alike

∴ By the Limit Comparison Theorem,

$\displaystyle\int_{1}^{\infty}\frac{\sqrt{x^7-5}}{x^4}\,dx$ also $\boxed{\text{Diverges}}$

SECTION III

3.1 Let $y(x)$ be the solution of the differential equation

$$x^3 \frac{dy}{dx} + 2y = e^{1/x^2} \quad \text{with } y(1) = e$$

Find $y\left(\dfrac{1}{2}\right)$.

(A) $\dfrac{4}{e^4}$ (E) $\dfrac{1}{2e^4}$

(B) $\dfrac{-1}{2}e^4$ (F) $\dfrac{1}{4e^4}$

(C) $\dfrac{-2}{3}e^4$ (G) $\dfrac{-3}{2}e^4$

(D) $\dfrac{1}{e^4}$ (H) $\dfrac{-3}{4}e^4$

3.1 Let $y(x)$ be the solution of the differential equation

$$x^3 \frac{dy}{dx} + 2y = e^{1/x^2} \quad \text{with } y(1) = e$$

Find $y\left(\dfrac{1}{2}\right)$.

(A) $\dfrac{4}{e^4}$ (E) $\dfrac{1}{2e^4}$

(B) $\dfrac{-1}{2}e^4$ (F) $\dfrac{1}{4e^4}$

(C) $\dfrac{-2}{3}e^4$ (G) $\dfrac{-3}{2}e^4$

(D) $\dfrac{1}{e^4}$ (H) $\dfrac{-3}{4}e^4$

This is a linear differential equation.

① Put the equation in Standard form.

$$\frac{dy}{dx} + P(x) \cdot y = Q(x)$$

Divide by x^3 to get

$$\frac{dy}{dx} + \underbrace{\frac{2}{x^3}}_{P(x)} y = \frac{e^{1/x^2}}{x^3}$$

② Find the integrating factor $M = e^{\int P(x)dx}$

$$\int P(x)dx = \int \frac{2}{x^3}dx = \int 2x^{-3}dx = \frac{2x^{-2}}{-2} = \frac{-1}{x^2}$$

$$M = e^{\int P(x)dx} = e^{\frac{-1}{x^2}}$$

③ Mult. the standard form equation by M

$$e^{\frac{-1}{x^2}} \cdot \frac{dy}{dx} + e^{\frac{-1}{x^2}} \cdot \frac{2}{x^3} y = \frac{e^{1/x^2}}{x^3} \cdot e^{-1/x^2}$$

④ Recognize LHS as $\frac{d}{dx}(M \cdot y)$

$$\frac{d}{dx}\left(\underbrace{e^{\frac{-1}{x^2}} \cdot y}_{M}\right) = \frac{1}{x^3}$$

⑤ Integrate both sides with respect to x

$$\int \frac{d}{dx}(e^{\frac{-1}{x^2}} \cdot y) dx = \int x^{-3}dx$$

$$e^{\frac{-1}{x^2}} \cdot y = \frac{x^{-2}}{-2} + C$$

$$e^{\frac{-1}{x^2}} \cdot y = \frac{-1}{2x^2} + C$$

⑥ Plug in the initial condition and solve for C $y(1) = e$

$$e^{\frac{-1}{x^2}} \cdot y = \frac{-1}{2x^2} + C$$

$$e^{-1} \cdot e = \frac{-1}{2} + C$$

$$1 = -\frac{1}{2} + C \Rightarrow C = \frac{3}{2}$$

$$e^{\frac{-1}{x^2}} \cdot y = \frac{-1}{2x^2} + \frac{3}{2}$$

⑦ Find $y\left(\frac{1}{2}\right)$

$$e^{-4} \cdot y = \frac{-1}{2 \cdot \frac{1}{4}} + \frac{3}{2}$$

$$y = \left(-2 + \frac{3}{2}\right)e^4$$

$$\boxed{y = -\frac{1}{2}e^4}$$

114

3.2 Let $y(x)$ be the solution of the differential equation

$$\frac{x}{y+2}\cdot\frac{dy}{dx}=\frac{1}{x+1} \quad \text{with } y\left(\frac{1}{2}\right)=1$$

Find $y(1)$.

(A) $\dfrac{1}{2}$　　(E) $\dfrac{9}{2}$

(B) $\dfrac{3}{2}$　　(F) 2

(C) $\dfrac{5}{2}$　　(G) 1

(D) $\dfrac{7}{2}$　　(H) $\dfrac{3}{4}$

3.2 Let $y(x)$ be the solution of the differential equation

$$\frac{x}{y+2}\cdot\frac{dy}{dx}=\frac{1}{x+1}\quad\text{with }y\left(\frac{1}{2}\right)=1$$

Find $y(1)$.

(A) $\dfrac{1}{2}$ (E) $\dfrac{9}{2}$

(B) $\dfrac{3}{2}$ (F) 2

(C) $\dfrac{5}{2}$ (G) 1

(D) $\dfrac{7}{2}$ (H) $\dfrac{3}{4}$

This equation is Separable.

① Use algebra to get
y's and | x's and
dy | dx
on LHS | on RHS

$$\frac{1}{y+2}\,dy = \frac{1}{x+1}\cdot\frac{1}{x}\,dx$$

② Integrate both sides   use Partial Fractions

$$\int\frac{1}{y+2}\,dy = \int\frac{1}{x(x+1)}\,dx$$

$$\int\frac{1}{y+2}\,dy = \int\left(\frac{A}{x}+\frac{B}{x+1}\right)\,dx$$

$A(x+1)+Bx = 1$
let $x=0$ $A=1$
let $x=-1$ $-B=1$
$B=-1$

$$\int\frac{1}{y+2}\,dy = \int\left(\frac{1}{x}-\frac{1}{x+1}\right)\,dx$$

$$\ln|y+2| = \ln|x| - \ln|x+1| + C$$

③ Plug in the initial condition to solve for C
$$y(\tfrac{1}{2})=1 \Rightarrow x=\tfrac{1}{2} \text{ & } y=1$$

$$\ln 3 = \ln|\tfrac{1}{2}| - \ln|\tfrac{3}{2}| + C$$
$$\ln 3 = \ln|\tfrac{1/2}{3/2}| + C$$
$$\ln 3 = \ln(\tfrac{1}{3}) + C$$
$$C = \ln 3 - \ln\tfrac{1}{3} \qquad \Rightarrow \underline{C=\ln 9}$$
$$\tfrac{3}{1/3}=9$$

④ Find $y(1)$
$$\ln|y+2| = \ln|x| - \ln|x+1| + \ln 9$$
$$\ln|y+2| = \ln 1 - \ln 2 + \ln 9$$
$$\ln|y+2| = \ln(\tfrac{9}{2})$$
$$e^{\ln|y+2|} = e^{\ln(9/2)} \Rightarrow y+2 = \tfrac{9}{2}$$
$$y = \tfrac{9}{2}-2$$
$$\boxed{y = 5/2}$$

116

3.3 Let $y(x)$ be the solution of the differential equation

$$\sqrt{\frac{x}{y}}\,\frac{dy}{dx} = \ln x \quad \text{with } y(1) = 9$$

Find $y(e^2)$.

(A) 2   (C) 3   (E) 4   (G) 8

(B) 10   (D) 16   (F) 25   (H) $2\sqrt{5}$

3.3 Let $y(x)$ be the solution of the differential equation

$$\sqrt{\frac{x}{y}}\frac{dy}{dx} = \ln x \quad \text{with } y(1) = 9$$

Find $y(e^2)$.

(A) 2   (C) 3   (E) 4   (G) 8

(B) 10   (D) 16   (F) 25   (H) $2\sqrt{5}$

The equation is separable.

① use algebra to get
     y's and | x's and
      dy | dx
   on LHS | on RHS

$$\frac{\sqrt{x}}{\sqrt{y}}\frac{dy}{dx} = \ln x$$

$$\frac{1}{\sqrt{y}}dy = \frac{\ln x}{\sqrt{x}}dx$$

② Integrate both sides   ⟵ Integrate by Parts

$$\int y^{-1/2}dy = \int \frac{\ln x}{\sqrt{x}}dx \qquad \begin{array}{l} u = \ln x \quad dv = x^{-1/2} \\ du = \frac{1}{x}dx \quad v = 2\sqrt{x} \end{array}$$

$$2y^{1/2} = 2\sqrt{x}\ln x - 4\sqrt{x} + C \qquad \begin{array}{l} uv - \int v\,du \\ 2\sqrt{x}\ln x - 2\int x^{-1/2}dx \\ 2\sqrt{x}\ln x - 4\sqrt{x} \end{array}$$

③ Plug in the initial condition to find C
   $y(1) = 9$ $x = 1$ $y = 9$

$$2\sqrt{9} = 2\sqrt{1}\cdot\ln 1 - 4\sqrt{1} + C$$
$$6 = 2\cdot 0 - 4 + C$$
$$\underline{\underline{10 = C}}$$

$$2\sqrt{y} = 2\sqrt{x}\ln x - 4\sqrt{x} + 10$$

④ Find $y(e^2)$

$$2\sqrt{y} = 2\sqrt{e^2}\cdot\ln e^2 - 4\sqrt{e^2} + 10$$
$$2\sqrt{y} = 2e\cdot 2 - 4e + 10$$
$$2\sqrt{y} = \cancel{4e} - \cancel{4e} + 10$$
$$\sqrt{y} = 5 \Rightarrow \boxed{y = 25}$$
      square both sides

3.4 Let $y(x)$ be the solution of the differertial equation

$$(x^2+1)\frac{dy}{dx}+3xy=3x \quad \text{with } y(0)=3$$

Find $y\left(\sqrt{3}\right)$

(A) $\dfrac{13}{8}$ (C) $\dfrac{3}{2}$ (E) $\dfrac{7}{4}$ (G) $\dfrac{5}{3}$

(B) $\dfrac{1}{2}$ (D) $\dfrac{5}{4}$ (F) $\dfrac{11}{6}$ (H) $\dfrac{11}{8}$

3.4 Let $y(x)$ be the solution of the differential equation

$$\left(x^2 + 1\right)\frac{dy}{dx} + 3xy = 3x \quad \text{with } y(0) = 3$$

Find $y\left(\sqrt{3}\right)$

(A) $\dfrac{13}{8}$ (C) $\dfrac{3}{2}$ (E) $\dfrac{7}{4}$ (G) $\dfrac{5}{3}$

(B) $\dfrac{1}{2}$ (D) $\dfrac{5}{4}$ (F) $\dfrac{11}{6}$ (H) $\dfrac{11}{8}$

The equation is both separable and linear.
Let's do this as linear.

$$\frac{dy}{dx} + \underbrace{\frac{3x}{x^2+1}}_{P(x)} y = \frac{3x}{x^2+1}$$

Find $\mu = e^{\int P(x)dx}$

$$\int \frac{3x}{x^2+1}dx \qquad \begin{array}{l} u = x^2+1 \\ du = 2x\,dx \\ \frac{1}{2}du = x\,dx \end{array} \qquad \begin{array}{l} \frac{3}{2}\int \frac{1}{u}du \\ = \frac{3}{2}\ln u \\ = \frac{3}{2}\ln(x^2+1) \end{array}$$

$$\mu = e^{\int P(x)dx} = e^{\frac{3}{2}\ln(x^2+1)} = e^{\ln(x^2+1)^{3/2}} = \left(x^2+1\right)^{3/2}$$

$$\left(x^2+1\right)^{3/2}\frac{dy}{dx} + \frac{3x}{x^2+1}\left(x^2+1\right)^{3/2} \cdot y = \frac{3x}{x^2+1}\left(x^2+1\right)^{3/2}$$

$$\frac{d}{dx}\left(\left(x^2+1\right)^{3/2} \cdot y\right) = 3x\sqrt{x^2+1} \qquad \begin{array}{l} u = x^2+1 \\ du = 2x\,dx \\ \frac{1}{2}du = x\,dx \end{array}$$

$$\int \frac{d}{dx}\left(\left(x^2+1\right)^{3/2} \cdot y\right)dx = \int 3x\sqrt{x^2+1}\,dx \qquad \begin{array}{l} \frac{3}{2}\int u^{1/2}du \\ \frac{3}{2} \cdot \frac{2}{3} u^{3/2} \end{array}$$

$$\left(x^2+1\right)^{3/2} \cdot y = \left(x^2+1\right)^{3/2} + C$$

$y(0) = 3 \qquad 1 \cdot 3 = 1 + C \Rightarrow \underline{C = 2}$

$$y = 1 + \frac{2}{\left(x^2+1\right)^{3/2}}$$

Find $y(\sqrt{3})$

$$y = 1 + \frac{2}{\left(\left(\sqrt{3}\right)^2+1\right)^{3/2}} = 1 + \frac{2}{4^{3/2}} = 1 + \frac{2}{2^3}$$

$$y = 1 + \frac{1}{2^2} = 1 + \frac{1}{4} \Rightarrow \boxed{y = \frac{5}{4}}$$

3.5 SET UP (but DO NOT SOLVE) the differential equation for the word problem. Give the differential equation and the initial condition.

A tank initially holds 700 gallons of brine with 12 lbs. of dissolved salt.
Brine that contains 5 lbs. of salt per gallon enters the tank at the rate of 4 gallons per minute and the well stirred mixture leaves at the rate of 7 gallons per minute. Let $y(t)$ be amount of salt in the tank at time t. Find the differential equation and initial condition.

3.5 SET UP (but DO NOT SOLVE) the differential equation for the word problem. Give the differential equation and the initial condition.

A tank initially holds 700 gallons of brine with 12 lbs. of dissolved salt.
Brine that contains 5 lbs. of salt per gallon enters the tank at the rate of 4 gallons per minute and the well stirred mixture leaves at the rate of 7 gallons per minute. Let $y(t)$ be amount of salt in the tank at time t. Find the differential equation and initial condition.

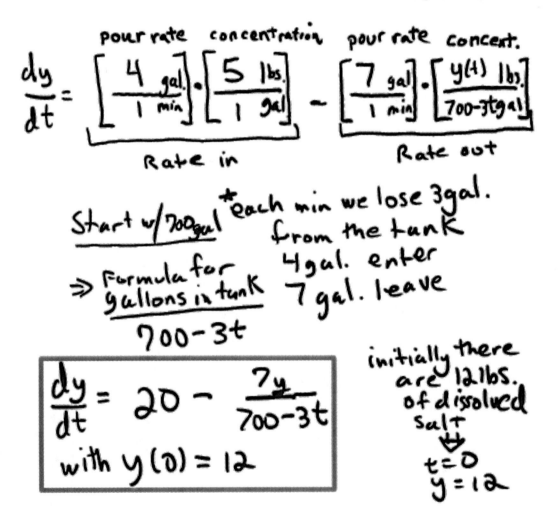

$$\frac{dy}{dt} = \underbrace{\left[\overset{\text{pour rate}}{\frac{4 \text{ gal.}}{1 \text{ min}}}\right]\cdot\left[\overset{\text{concentration}}{\frac{5 \text{ lbs.}}{1 \text{ gal}}}\right]}_{\text{Rate in}} - \underbrace{\left[\overset{\text{pour rate}}{\frac{7 \text{ gal}}{1 \text{ min}}}\right]\cdot\left[\overset{\text{concent.}}{\frac{y(t) \text{ lbs.}}{700-3t \text{ gal}}}\right]}_{\text{Rate out}}$$

Start w/ 700gal * each min we lose 3gal. from the tank
4 gal. enter
7 gal. leave

⇒ Formula for gallons in tank
$$700-3t$$

$$\boxed{\frac{dy}{dt} = 20 - \frac{7y}{700-3t}}$$
$$\text{with } y(0) = 12$$

initially there are 12 lbs. of dissolved salt
↓
$t = 0$
$y = 12$

122

3.6 Let $y(x)$ be the solution of the differential equation

$xy' - \ln x = 0$ with $y(1) = \dfrac{7}{2}$

Find $y(e)$.

(A) 0   (E) 2

(B) e (F) 3

(C) $\dfrac{1}{2}$ (G) 4

(D) 1   (H) 5

3.6 Let $y(x)$ be the solution of the differential equation

$xy' - \ln x = 0$ with $y(1) = \dfrac{7}{2}$

Find $y(e)$.

(A) 0   (E) 2

(B) e (F) 3

(C) $\dfrac{1}{2}$ (G) 4

(D) 1   (H) 5

The equation is separable.

$$xy' = \ln x$$

$$\frac{dy}{dx} = \frac{\ln x}{x} \Rightarrow dy = \frac{\ln x}{x} dx$$

Now integrate

$$\int dy = \int \frac{\ln x}{x} dx \qquad u = \ln x$$
$$\qquad\qquad\qquad du = \frac{1}{x} du$$
$$y = \frac{1}{2}(\ln x)^2 + C \qquad \int u\,du = \frac{u^2}{2}$$

Now plug in initial cond. to find C

$$y(1) = 7/2 \Rightarrow x = 1 \quad y = 7/2$$

$$\frac{7}{2} = \frac{1}{2}(\ln 1)^2 + C \Rightarrow C = \frac{7}{2}$$
$$\qquad\qquad \underset{0}{\underbrace{\quad}}$$

$$y = \frac{1}{2}(\ln x)^2 + \frac{7}{2}$$

Find $y(e)$

$$y = \frac{1}{2}(\ln e)^2 + \frac{7}{2} \Rightarrow y = \frac{1}{2} + \frac{7}{2}$$
$$\qquad\qquad\underset{1}{\underbrace{\quad}}$$

$$\boxed{y(e) = 4}$$

3.7 Let $y(x)$ be the solution of the differential equation

$$xy' + \frac{1}{2}y = x^{3/2} \quad \text{with } y(1) = \frac{5}{2}$$

Find $y(4)$.

(A) 0   (E) 2

(B) e (F) 3

(C) $\dfrac{1}{2}$ (G) 4

(D) 1   (H) 5

3.7 Let $y(x)$ be the solution of the differertial equation

$$xy' + \frac{1}{2}y = x^{3/2} \quad \text{with } y(1) = \frac{5}{2}$$

Find $y(4)$.

(A) 0   (E) 2

(B) e (F) 3

(C) $\dfrac{1}{2}$ (G) 4

(D) 1   (H) 5

The equation is linear. Divide by x to put the eq. in std. form

Standard form:

$$\frac{dy}{dx} + \frac{1}{2} \cdot \frac{1}{x} \cdot y = \frac{x^{3/2}}{x}$$

$$\frac{dy}{dx} + \left[\frac{1}{2} \cdot \frac{1}{x}\right] y = x^{1/2}$$

$$\underbrace{\phantom{\left[\frac{1}{2} \cdot \frac{1}{x}\right]}}_{P(x)}$$

$$M = e^{\int P(x)dx} = e^{\int \frac{1}{2} \cdot \frac{1}{x}dx} = e^{\frac{1}{2}\int \frac{1}{x}dx}$$

$$M = e^{\frac{1}{2}\ln x} = e^{\ln x^{1/2}} = x^{1/2}$$

$$x^{1/2} \cdot \frac{dy}{dx} + \frac{1}{2x} \cdot x^{1/2} \, y = x^{1/2} \cdot x^{1/2}$$

$$\underbrace{\phantom{x^{1/2} \cdot \frac{dy}{dx} + \frac{1}{2x} \cdot x^{1/2} \, y}}$$

$$\frac{d}{dx}\left[\underset{M}{x^{1/2}} \cdot \underset{y}{y}\right] = x \quad \text{Now integrate}$$

$$\int \frac{d}{dx}[x^{1/2} \cdot y] \, dx = \int x \, dx$$

$$x^{1/2} \cdot y = \frac{x^2}{2} + C$$

Plug in initial condition to find C

$$y(1) = \frac{5}{2} \quad x = 1 \quad y = \frac{5}{2}$$

$$1 \cdot \frac{5}{2} = \frac{1}{2} + C \Rightarrow C = \frac{5}{2} - \frac{1}{2} = 2$$

$$\sqrt{x} \cdot y = \frac{x^2}{2} + 2$$

Find $y(4)$.

$$\sqrt{4} \cdot y = \frac{4^2}{2} + 2 \Rightarrow 2y = \frac{8 + 2}{10}$$

$$\boxed{y(4) = 5}$$

126

3.8 Let $y(x)$ be the solution of the differential equation

$$\frac{dy}{dx} - xe^{-y} = 2e^{-y} \text{ with } y(0) = 0$$

Find $y(1)$.

(A) $\ln 2$ (C) $\ln\left(\dfrac{5}{2}\right)$ (E) $\ln\left(\dfrac{3}{2}\right)$ (G) $\ln\left(\dfrac{9}{2}\right)$

(B) 1 (D) $\ln\left(\dfrac{7}{2}\right)$ (F) $\ln 3$ (H) $2\ln 5$

3.8 Let $y(x)$ be the solution of the differertial equation

$$\frac{dy}{dx} - xe^{-y} = 2e^{-y} \text{ with } y(0) = 0$$

Find $y(1)$.

(A) $\ln 2$

(C) $\ln\left(\frac{5}{2}\right)$

(E) $\ln\left(\frac{3}{2}\right)$

(G) $\ln\left(\frac{9}{2}\right)$

(B) 1

(D) $\ln\left(\frac{7}{2}\right)$

(F) $\ln 3$

(H) $2\ln 5$

The equation is separable. Solve for $\frac{dy}{dx}$

$$\frac{dy}{dx} = 2e^{-y} + xe^{-y} \quad \text{Factor out } e^{-y}$$

$$\frac{dy}{dx} = e^{-y}(2+x) \Rightarrow \frac{dy}{dx} = \frac{2+x}{e^y}$$

$$e^y dy = (2+x) dx \quad \text{Now integrate}$$

$$\int e^y dy = \int (2+x) dx$$

$$e^y = 2x + \frac{x^2}{2} + C \quad \text{Plug in the initial cond}$$

$$e^0 = 0 + 0 + C \qquad \begin{array}{l} y(0) = 0 \\ \Rightarrow C = 1 \end{array}$$

$$e^y = 2x + \frac{x^2}{2} + 1 \qquad \text{Find } y(1)$$

$$e^y = 2 + \frac{1}{2} + 1 \Rightarrow e^y = \frac{7}{2}$$

$$\ln(e^y) = \ln\left(\frac{7}{2}\right) \qquad \boxed{y(1) = \ln\left(\frac{7}{2}\right)}$$

3.9 Show that $x(1 + \sin x) = O(3x)$. Explain using a limit.

$$\uparrow$$

$$\text{big } O$$

3.9 Show that $x(1 + \sin x) = O(3x)$. Explain using a limit.

↑

big O

$$f(x) = O(g(x)) \text{ if } \lim_{x \to \infty} \frac{f(x)}{g(x)} \le M$$

- M positive constant
- for sufficiently large x

$$\lim_{x \to \infty} \frac{x(1+\sin x)}{3x} = \frac{1 + \sin x}{3} \le \frac{1+1}{3} = \frac{2}{3}$$

$-1 \le \sin x \le 1$

So $\lim_{x \to \infty} \frac{x(1+\sin x)}{3x} \le \frac{2}{3}$

↗

M

∴ $\boxed{x(1+\sin x) = O(3x)}$

3.10 Show that $\sqrt{x^3 + 4x} = o\left(x^2\right)$. Explain using a limit.

$$\uparrow$$

little o

3.10 Show that $\sqrt{x^3 + 4x} = o\left(x^2\right)$. Explain using a limit.

$\uparrow$

little o

$$f(x) = o(g(x)) \text{ if } \lim_{x \to \infty} \frac{f(x)}{g(x)} = 0$$

$$\lim_{x \to \infty} \frac{\sqrt{x^3 + 4x}}{x^2} \cdot \frac{\frac{1}{x^2}}{\frac{1}{x^2}} = \lim_{x \to \infty} \frac{\frac{\sqrt{x^3 + 4x}}{x^2}}{1}$$

$$= \lim_{x \to \infty} \frac{\sqrt{x^3 + 4x}}{\sqrt{x^4}} = \lim_{x \to \infty} \sqrt{\frac{x^3 + 4x}{x^4}}$$

$$= \lim_{x \to \infty} \sqrt{\frac{1}{x} + \frac{4}{x^3}} = \sqrt{\lim_{x \to \infty} \frac{1}{x} + \lim_{x \to \infty} \frac{4}{x^3}} = 0$$

$\underset{\to 0}{\underbrace{\qquad}} \quad \underset{\to 0}{\underbrace{\qquad}}$

3.11 Which function grows faster: $f(x) = 3^x$ or $g(x) = 2^{x+2}$?
Explain using a limit.

3.11 Which function grows faster: $f(x) = 3^x$ or $g(x) = 2^{x+2}$?

Explain using a limit.

If $\lim\limits_{x \to \infty} \dfrac{f(x)}{g(x)} = 0$, then $g(x)$ grows faster than $f(x)$

If $\lim\limits_{x \to \infty} \dfrac{f(x)}{g(x)} = \infty$, then $f(x)$ grows faster than $g(x)$

$$\lim_{x \to \infty} \frac{3^x}{2^{x+2}} = \lim_{x \to \infty} \frac{3^x}{2^x \cdot 2} = \frac{1}{2} \underbrace{\lim_{x \to \infty} \left(\frac{3}{2}\right)^x}_{\to \infty}$$

$\to \infty$

since

$\dfrac{3}{2} > 1$

So $\boxed{3^x \text{ grows faster than } 2^{x+2}}$

3.12 Which function grows faster: $f(x) = \ln x$ or $g(x) = \sqrt{x}$? Explain using limits.

3.12 Which function grows faster: $f(x) = \ln x$ or $g(x) = \sqrt{x}$? Explain using limits.

If $\displaystyle\lim_{x \to \infty} \frac{f(x)}{g(x)} = 0$, then $g(x)$ grows faster than $f(x)$

If $\displaystyle\lim_{x \to \infty} \frac{f(x)}{g(x)} = \infty$, then $f(x)$ grows faster than $g(x)$

$$\lim_{x \to \infty} \frac{\ln x}{\sqrt{x}} = \text{"}\frac{\infty}{\infty}\text{"} \quad \text{use L'Hôpital's Rule}$$

$$\stackrel{L'H}{=} \lim_{x \to \infty} \frac{\frac{1}{x}}{\frac{1}{2\sqrt{x}}} = \lim_{x \to \infty} \frac{1}{x} \cdot \frac{2\sqrt{x}}{1} = \lim_{x \to \infty} \frac{2}{\sqrt{x}} = 0$$

So, $\boxed{\sqrt{x} \text{ grows faster than } \ln x}$

3.13 Which function grows faster: $f(x) = x^{100}$ or $g(x) = e^x$?
Explain using limits.

3.13 Which function grows faster: $f(x) = x^{100}$ or $g(x) = e^x$?
Explain using limits.

If $\lim\limits_{x \to \infty} \dfrac{f(x)}{g(x)} = 0$, then $g(x)$ grows faster than $f(x)$

If $\lim\limits_{x \to \infty} \dfrac{f(x)}{g(x)} = \infty$, then $f(x)$ grows faster than $g(x)$

$$\lim\limits_{x \to \infty} \dfrac{x^{100}}{e^x} = \text{``} \dfrac{\infty}{\infty} \text{''} \overset{L'H}{=} \lim\limits_{x \to \infty} \dfrac{100 x^{99}}{e^x} \overset{L'H}{=} \lim\limits_{x \to \infty} \dfrac{100 \cdot 99 x^{98}}{e^x}$$

Do this 98 more times to obtain

$$\lim\limits_{x \to \infty} \dfrac{100!}{e^x} = 0$$

So, $\boxed{e^x \text{ grows faster than } x^{100}}$

138

3.14 Determine the limit of the sequence

$$a_n = \left\{ \sqrt{n^2 + 3n} - n \right\}$$

(A) 3   (B) 2   (C) 1 / 2   (D) 3 / 2

(E) 0   (F) 1   (G) ∞ (H) does not exist

3.14 Determine the limit of the sequence

$$a_n = \left\{ \sqrt{n^2 + 3n} - n \right\}$$

(A) 3   (B) 2   (C) $1/2$ (D) $3/2$

(E) 0   (F) 1   (G) ∞ (H) does not exist

Multiply by the conjugate

$$\lim_{n \to \infty} \frac{\sqrt{n^2+3n}-n}{1} \cdot \frac{\sqrt{n^2+3n}+n}{\sqrt{n^2+3n}+n} = \lim_{n \to \infty} \frac{\cancel{n^2}+3n-\cancel{n^2}}{\sqrt{n^2+3n}+n}$$

$$= \lim_{n \to \infty} \frac{3n}{\sqrt{n^2+3n}+n} \cdot \frac{\frac{1}{n}}{\frac{1}{n}} = \lim_{n \to \infty} \frac{3}{\frac{\sqrt{n^2+3n}}{n}+1}$$

$$\uparrow$$
rename to $\sqrt{n^2}$

$$= \lim_{n \to \infty} \frac{3}{\sqrt{\frac{n^2+3n}{n^2}}+1}$$

$$= \lim_{n \to \infty} \frac{3}{\sqrt{1+\underbrace{\frac{3}{n}}_{\to 0 \text{ as } n \to \infty}}+1} = \frac{3}{\sqrt{1}+1} = \boxed{\frac{3}{2}}$$

3.15 Determine the limit of the sequence

$$a_n = \left\{ \frac{e^n}{1 + e^{-n}} \right\}$$

3.15 Determine the limit of the sequence

$$a_n = \left\{ \frac{e^n}{1 + e^{-n}} \right\}$$

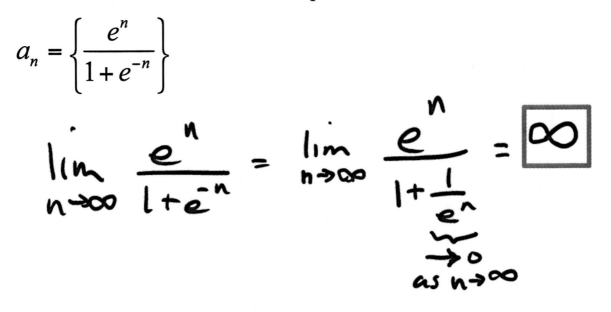

$$\lim_{n \to \infty} \frac{e^n}{1 + e^{-n}} = \lim_{n \to \infty} \frac{e^n}{1 + \frac{1}{e^n}} = \boxed{\infty}$$

$$\frac{1}{e^n} \to 0 \quad \text{as } n \to \infty$$

3.16 Determine the limit of the sequence

$$a_n = \left\{ \left(2 + \frac{n^2}{2} \right)^{\frac{1}{\ln(2n)}} \right\}$$

(A) ∞　　　　(B) $\dfrac{1}{e}$　　　　(C) e^2　　　　(D) 0

(E) 1　　　　(F) e　　　　(G) $\dfrac{1}{e^2}$　　　　(H) $\sqrt{e}$

3.16 Determine the limit of the sequence

$$a_n = \left\{ \left(2 + \frac{n^2}{2} \right)^{\frac{1}{\ln(2n)}} \right\}$$

(A) ∞ (B) $\dfrac{1}{e}$ (C) e^2 (D) 0

(E) 1 (F) e (G) $\dfrac{1}{e^2}$ (H) $\sqrt{e}$

$$\lim_{n\to\infty} \left(2 + \frac{n^2}{2} \right)^{\frac{1}{\ln 2n}} = \infty^{0} \quad \text{"}\;\text{"} \quad \text{indeterminant power}$$

$$y = \lim_{n\to\infty} \left(2 + \frac{n^2}{2} \right)^{\frac{1}{\ln(2n)}} \qquad \text{take } \ln$$

$$\ln y = \lim_{n\to\infty} \ln\left[\left(2 + \frac{n^2}{2} \right)^{\frac{1}{\ln(2n)}} \right]$$

$$\ln y = \lim_{n\to\infty} \frac{1}{\ln(2n)} \cdot \ln\left(2 + \frac{n^2}{2} \right) = 0 \cdot \infty \quad \text{"}\;\text{"}$$

$$\ln y = \lim_{n\to\infty} \frac{\ln\left(2 + \frac{n^2}{2} \right)}{\ln(2n)} = \frac{\infty}{\infty} \quad \text{"}\;\text{"} \quad \text{use L'Hôpital's Rule}$$

$$\ln y \overset{L'H}{=} \lim_{n\to\infty} \frac{\dfrac{1}{2 + \frac{n^2}{2}} \cdot n}{\dfrac{1}{2n} \cdot 2} = \lim_{n\to\infty} \frac{\dfrac{n}{2 + \frac{n^2}{2}}}{\dfrac{1}{n}}$$

$$\ln y = \lim_{n\to\infty} \frac{n}{2 + \frac{n^2}{2}} \cdot \frac{n}{1} = \lim_{n\to\infty} \frac{n^2}{2 + \frac{n^2}{2}} \cdot \frac{\frac{1}{n^2}}{\frac{1}{n^2}} = \lim_{n\to\infty} \frac{1}{\frac{2}{n^2} + \frac{1}{2}} = 2$$

$$\underset{\to 0}{\underbrace{\phantom{\frac{2}{n^2}}}}$$

$$\ln y = 2 \qquad e^{\ln y} = e^2 \;\Rightarrow\; y = e^2$$

$$\boxed{\lim_{n\to\infty} \left(2 + \frac{n^2}{2} \right)^{\frac{1}{\ln(2n)}} = e^2}$$

3.17 Determine the limit of the sequence

$$a_n = \left\{ \left(\frac{n+2}{n-2} \right)^n \right\}$$

(A) e (C) e^4 (E) 2   (G) 0

(B) e^2 (D) 1   (F) 4   (H) ∞

3.17 Determine the limit of the sequence

$$a_n = \left\{ \left(\frac{n+2}{n-2} \right)^n \right\}$$

(A) e (C) e^4 (E) 2   (G) 0

(B) e^2 (D) 1   (F) 4   (H) ∞

$\lim\limits_{n \to \infty} \left(\frac{n+2}{n-2} \right)^n = \text{``} 1^{\infty} \text{''}$ Indeterminant Power

$y = \lim\limits_{n \to \infty} \left(\frac{n+2}{n-2} \right)^n$ Take $\ln$ of both sides

$\ln y = \lim\limits_{n \to \infty} \ln \left(\frac{n+2}{n-2} \right)^n$

$\ln y = \lim\limits_{n \to \infty} n \cdot \ln \left(\frac{n+2}{n-2} \right) = \text{``} \infty \cdot 0 \text{''}$

$\ln y = \lim\limits_{n \to \infty} \dfrac{\ln \left(\frac{n+2}{n-2} \right)}{\frac{1}{n}} = \text{``} \frac{0}{0} \text{''}$

Before using L'Hôpital's Rule, simplify

$\ln y = \lim\limits_{n \to \infty} \dfrac{\ln(n+2) - \ln(n-2)}{\frac{1}{n}}$

$\ln y \overset{L'H}{=} \lim\limits_{n \to \infty} \dfrac{\frac{1}{n+2} - \frac{1}{n-2}}{\frac{-1}{n^2}} = \lim\limits_{n \to \infty} \dfrac{\frac{n-2-(n+2)}{n^2-4}}{\frac{-1}{n^2}}$

$\ln y = \lim\limits_{n \to \infty} \dfrac{-4}{n^2-4} \cdot \dfrac{-n^2}{1} = \lim\limits_{n \to \infty} \dfrac{4n^2}{n^2-4} = 4$

$\ln y = 4$

$e^{\ln y} = e^4 \implies y = e^4$

deg num = deg den so the limit is the ratio of coeff on highest deg. terms

$$\boxed{\lim\limits_{n \to \infty} \left(\frac{n+2}{n-2} \right)^n = e^4}$$

3.18 Determine the limit of the sequence

$$a_n = \left\{ \frac{n}{2} \sin\left(\frac{2}{n} \right) \right\}$$

3.18 Determine the limit of the sequence

$$a_n = \left\{ \frac{n}{2} \sin\left(\frac{2}{n}\right) \right\}$$

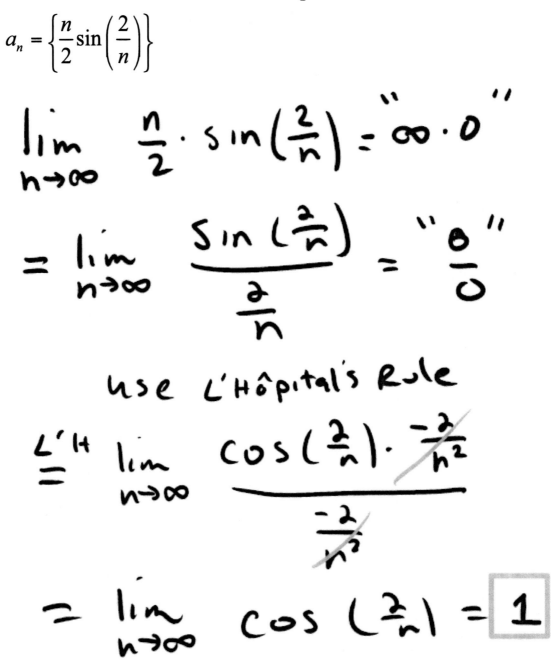

$$\lim_{n \to \infty} \frac{n}{2} \cdot \sin\left(\frac{2}{n}\right) = "\infty \cdot 0"$$

$$= \lim_{n \to \infty} \frac{\sin\left(\frac{2}{n}\right)}{\frac{2}{n}} = "\frac{0}{0}"$$

use L'Hôpital's Rule

$$\overset{L'H}{=} \lim_{n \to \infty} \frac{\cos\left(\frac{2}{n}\right) \cdot \frac{-2}{n^2}}{\frac{-2}{n^2}}$$

$$= \lim_{n \to \infty} \cos\left(\frac{2}{n}\right) = \boxed{1}$$

3.19 Determine whether the series converges or diverges.

If it converges, find its sum.

$$\sum_{n=4}^{\infty} \frac{4}{n^2 - 1}$$

3.19 Determine whether the series converges or diverges. If it converges, find its sum.

$$\sum_{n=4}^{\infty} \frac{4}{n^2-1}$$

$n^2-1 = (n+1)(n-1)$ use partial fractions

$$\sum_{n=4}^{\infty} \frac{4}{n^2-1} = \sum_{n=4}^{\infty}\left(\frac{A}{n+1} + \frac{B}{n-1}\right) \qquad A(n-1)+B(n+1)=4$$

$n=1: \quad 2B = 4 \Rightarrow B=2$

$n=-1 \quad -2A = 4 \Rightarrow A=-2$

$$= \sum_{n=4}^{\infty}\left(\frac{2}{n-1} - \frac{2}{n+1}\right) \qquad \text{Telescoping Series}$$

$$\lim_{n\to\infty} S_n = \lim_{n\to\infty} \left(\frac{2}{3} - \frac{2}{5}\right) + \left(\frac{2}{4} - \frac{2}{6}\right) + \left(\frac{2}{5} - \frac{2}{7}\right) + \ldots$$

$\qquad\qquad\qquad n=4 \qquad\qquad n=5 \qquad\qquad n=6$

$$\ldots \left(\frac{2}{n-3} - \frac{2}{n-1}\right) + \left(\frac{2}{n-2} - \frac{2}{n}\right) + \left(\frac{2}{n-1} - \frac{2}{n+1}\right)$$

$\qquad\qquad\quad n-2 \qquad\qquad\quad n-1 \qquad\qquad\quad n$

$\circ \ \frac{2}{5}$ was the first to cancel. Higher terms $\frac{2}{6}$ and $\frac{2}{7}$ will cancel

Mimic the first cancellation with the end terms

$\frac{2}{n-1}$ cancels. This is the final term to cancel.

Terms lower than it will cancel

$$\lim_{n\to\infty} S_n = \lim_{n\to\infty} \frac{2}{3} + \frac{2}{4} - \underbrace{\frac{2}{n} - \frac{2}{n+1}}_{\to 0 \text{ as } n\to\infty} = \frac{2}{3} + \frac{1}{2}$$

$$= \frac{4+3}{6}$$

$$\boxed{Sum = \frac{7}{6}}$$

3.20 Determine whether the series converges or diverges.
If it converges, find its sum.

$$\sum_{n=1}^{\infty}\left[\left(\frac{6}{7}\right)^{n}-\frac{3}{2^{n}}\right]$$

(A) converges, sum is 5   (B) converges, sum is 3   (C) converges, sum is 2

(D) converges, sum is 6   (E) converges, sum is 4   (F) converges, sum is 7

(G) diverges   (H) none of the above

3.20 Determine whether the series converges or diverges.
If it converges, find its sum.

$$\sum_{n=1}^{\infty}\left[\left(\frac{6}{7}\right)^{n}-\frac{3}{2^{n}}\right]$$

(A) converges, sum is 5   (B) converges, sum is 3   (C) converges, sum is 2

(D) converges, sum is 6   (E) converges, sum is 4   (F) converges, sum is 7

(G) diverges   (H) none of the above

$$=\sum_{n=1}^{\infty}\left(\frac{6}{7}\right)^{n}-\sum_{n=1}^{\infty}\frac{3}{2^{n}}$$ Two geometric
Series

$\underbrace{\qquad}_{Sum\,1}$ $\underbrace{\qquad}_{Sum\,2}$

★ $\underline{Sum\,1}$ $= \frac{6}{7}+\frac{36}{49}+\cdots$

first term $= \frac{6}{7}$

ratio $= \frac{6}{7}$ or r $|r|<1$ so the sum
Conv. to:

$Sum\,1 = \dfrac{\frac{6}{7}}{1-\frac{6}{7}} = \dfrac{\frac{6}{7}}{\frac{1}{7}} = \frac{6}{7}\cdot\frac{7}{1} = \boxed{6}$

★ $\underline{Sum\,2} = 3\cdot\sum_{n=1}^{\infty}\frac{1}{2^{n}} = 3\cdot\sum_{n=1}^{\infty}\left(\frac{1}{2}\right)^{n}$

first term $= 3\cdot\frac{1}{2}$

ratio $= \frac{1}{2}$ or r $|r|<1$ so the sum
conv. to:

$Sum\,2 = \dfrac{\frac{3}{2}}{1-\frac{1}{2}} = \frac{3}{2}\cdot\frac{2}{1} = \boxed{3}$
$\underbrace{\qquad}_{1/2}$

Answer: $Sum\,1 - Sum\,2$ (since they both conv.)

$6 - 3 = \boxed{3}$

152

3.21 Find the sum of the series

$$\sum_{n=1}^{\infty} \frac{1}{n(n+2)}$$

(A) 3 / 4   (B) 1 / 2   (C) 3 / 5   (D) 9 / 10

(E) 2 / 3   (F) 4 / 5   (G) divergent   (H) none of the above

3.21 Find the sum of the series

$$\sum_{n=1}^{\infty} \frac{1}{n(n+2)}$$

(A) $3/4$ (B) $1/2$ (C) $3/5$ (D) $9/10$

(E) $2/3$ (F) $4/5$ (G) divergent (H) none of the above

This is a telescoping series

$$= \sum_{n=1}^{\infty} \left(\frac{A}{n} + \frac{B}{n+2} \right) \quad A(n+2) + Bn = 1$$

$$n=0 \quad 2A = 1 \Rightarrow A = \tfrac{1}{2}$$
$$n=-2 \quad -2B = 1 \Rightarrow B = -\tfrac{1}{2}$$

$$= \sum_{n=1}^{\infty} \left(\frac{1/2}{n} - \frac{1/2}{n+2} \right)$$

$$\text{Sum} = \lim_{n\to\infty} S_n = \lim_{n\to\infty} \underbrace{\left(\frac{1/2}{1} - \frac{1/2}{3} \right)}_{n=1} + \underbrace{\left(\frac{1/2}{2} - \frac{1/2}{4} \right)}_{n=2} + \underbrace{\left(\frac{1/2}{3} - \frac{1/2}{5} \right)}_{} + \cdots /$$

$$+ \cdots / / \underbrace{\left(\frac{1/2}{n-2} - \frac{1/2}{n} \right)}_{n-2} + \underbrace{\left(\frac{1/2}{n-1} - \frac{1/2}{n+1} \right)}_{n-1} + \underbrace{\left(\frac{1/2}{n} - \frac{1/2}{n+2} \right)}_{n}$$

→ $\frac{1/2}{3}$ was the first to cancel. Higher terms $\frac{1/2}{4}$ and $\frac{1/2}{5}$ will cancel

Mimic the first cancellation with the end terms

$\frac{1/2}{n}$ cancels. This is the final term to cancel.

Terms lower than it will cancel.

$$\text{Sum} = \lim_{n\to\infty} \frac{1}{2} + \frac{1}{4} - \underbrace{\frac{1/2}{n+1} - \frac{1/2}{n+2}}_{\to 0 \text{ as } n\to\infty} = \frac{1}{2} + \frac{1}{4}$$

$$\boxed{\text{Sum} = \frac{3}{4}}$$

154

3.22 Determine whether the series converges or diverges.

If it converges, find its sum.

$$\sum_{n=1}^{\infty} \left[(0.6)^{n-1} - (0.2)^n \right]$$

3.22 Determine whether the series converges or diverges.
If it converges, find its sum.

$$\sum_{n=1}^{\infty}\left[(0.6)^{n-1}-(0.2)^{n}\right]$$

We have two geometric series

$$=\sum_{n=1}^{\infty}(0.6)^{n-1}-\sum_{n=1}^{\infty}(0.2)^{n}$$

$\underbrace{\phantom{\sum_{n=1}^{\infty}(0.6)^{n-1}}}_{\text{sum 1}}$ $\underbrace{\phantom{\sum_{n=1}^{\infty}(0.2)^{n}}}_{\text{sum 2}}$

★ sum 1 :

first term = 1

ratio = 0.6 ∈ r |r| < 1 so the
                        series conv. to:

$$Sum 1 = \frac{1}{1-0.6} = \frac{1}{0.4} = \frac{1}{\frac{4}{10}} = \frac{10}{4} = \boxed{\frac{5}{2}}$$

★ sum 2 :

first term = 0.2

ratio = 0.2 ∈ r |r| < 1 so the
                        series conv. to:

$$Sum 2 = \frac{0.2}{1-0.2} = \frac{0.2}{0.8} = \frac{2}{8} = \boxed{\frac{1}{4}}$$

The original series will conv. to:

$$Sum 1 - Sum 2 = \frac{5}{2} - \frac{1}{4} = \frac{10-1}{4}$$

$$\boxed{Sum = \frac{9}{4}}$$

3.23 Determine whether the series converges or diverges.

If it converges, find its sum.

$$\frac{1}{e^2} - \frac{2\pi}{e^5} + \frac{4\pi^2}{e^8} - \frac{8\pi^3}{e^{11}} + \cdots$$

3.23 Determine whether the series converges or diverges.
If it converges, find its sum.

$$\frac{1}{e^2} - \frac{2\pi}{e^5} + \frac{4\pi^2}{e^8} - \frac{8\pi^3}{e^{11}} + \cdots$$

$\times \frac{-2\pi}{e^3} \quad \times \frac{-2\pi}{e^3} \quad \times \frac{-2\pi}{e^3}$ Geometric Series

$$r = \frac{-2\pi}{e^3} \qquad |r| = \frac{2\pi}{e^3} < 1 \text{ since}$$

$$\underline{\text{Conv. to}} \qquad \begin{array}{c} 2\pi < e^3 \\ \sim 6 \quad \sim 9 \end{array}$$

$$\text{Sum} = \frac{\frac{1}{e^2}}{1 - \left(\frac{-2\pi}{e^3}\right)} = \frac{\frac{1}{e^2}}{1 + \frac{2\pi}{e^3}} \cdot \frac{e^3}{e^3} = \frac{e}{e^3 + 2\pi}$$

$$\boxed{\text{Sum} = \frac{e}{e^3 + 2\pi}}$$

158

3.24 Determine whether the series converges or diverges.

If it converges, find its sum.

$$\sum_{n=1}^{\infty} \left(\arccos\left(\frac{\sqrt{3}}{n+1} \right) - \arccos\left(\frac{\sqrt{3}}{n+2} \right) \right)$$

3.24 Determine whether the series converges or diverges. If it converges, find its sum.

$$\sum_{n=1}^{\infty}\left(\arccos\left(\frac{\sqrt{3}}{n+1} \right) - \arccos\left(\frac{\sqrt{3}}{n+2} \right) \right)$$

This is a telescoping series.

$$Sum = \lim_{n\to\infty} S_n = \left(\arccos \frac{\sqrt{3}}{2} - \arccos \frac{\sqrt{3}}{3} \right) + \left(\arccos \frac{\sqrt{3}}{3} - \arccos \frac{\sqrt{3}}{4} \right) + \cdots$$

$$\cdots + \left(\arccos \frac{\sqrt{3}}{n} - \arccos \frac{\sqrt{3}}{n+1} \right) + \left(\arccos \frac{\sqrt{3}}{n+1} - \arccos \frac{\sqrt{3}}{n+2} \right)$$

(with $n=1$, $n=2$, $n-1$, n labeling the terms)

★ $\arccos \frac{\sqrt{3}}{3}$ was the first to cancel. Higher term $\arccos \frac{\sqrt{3}}{4}$ will cancel

Mimic the first cancellation with the end terms

$\arccos \frac{\sqrt{3}}{n+1}$ cancels. This is the final term to cancel.

Terms lower than it will cancel.

$$Sum = \lim_{n\to\infty} \underbrace{\arccos \frac{\sqrt{3}}{2}}_{} - \arccos \underbrace{\frac{\sqrt{3}}{n+2}}_{\to 0 \text{ as } n\to\infty}$$

$$Sum = \frac{\pi}{6} - \frac{\pi}{2} = \frac{\pi - 3\pi}{6} = \frac{-2\pi}{6}$$

$$\boxed{Sum = -\frac{\pi}{3}}$$

3.25 Determine whether the series converges or diverges.

If it converges, find its sum.

$$10 - 6 + 3.6 - 2.16 + \cdots$$

3.25 Determine whether the series converges or diverges.
If it converges, find its sum.

$$10 - 6 + 3.6 - 2.16 + \cdots$$

The series doesn't look geometric but it could be

$$10 \cdot \boxed{r} = -6 \implies r = \frac{-6}{10} = \frac{-3}{5}$$

$$-6 \boxed{r} = 3.6 \qquad -6 \cdot \frac{-6}{10} = \frac{36}{10} = 3.6 \checkmark$$

$$3.6 \boxed{r} = -2.16 \qquad 3.6 \times \frac{-6}{10} = \frac{-21.6}{10} = -2.16 \checkmark$$

So the series is geometric with

$$r = \frac{-6}{10} \qquad |r| < 1 \implies \text{the series conv. to:}$$

first term = 10

$$\text{Sum} = \frac{10}{1 - \frac{-6}{10}} = \frac{10}{\frac{16}{10}} = \frac{100}{16}$$

$$\boxed{\text{Sum} = \frac{25}{4}}$$

SECTION IV

Convergence Tests
Power Series

4.1 Determine whether the series converges or diverges.

I. $\displaystyle\sum_{n=1}^{\infty}\left(n-\sqrt{n^2-5n}\right)$ II. $\displaystyle\sum_{n=1}^{\infty}(-1)^n\ln\left(1+\frac{2}{n^2}\right)$

4.1 Determine whether the series converges or diverges.

I. $\displaystyle\sum_{n=1}^{\infty}\left(n-\sqrt{n^2-5n}\right)$

II. $\displaystyle\sum_{n=1}^{\infty}(-1)^n \ln\left(1+\frac{2}{n^2}\right)$

I. Test for Divergence

$$\lim_{n\to\infty}\frac{n-\sqrt{n^2-5n}}{1}\cdot\frac{n+\sqrt{n^2-5n}}{n+\sqrt{n^2-5n}} = \lim_{n\to\infty}\frac{n^2-(n^2-5n)}{n+\sqrt{n^2-5n}}$$

$$= \lim_{n\to\infty}\frac{5n}{n+\sqrt{n^2-5n}}\cdot\frac{\frac{1}{n}}{\frac{1}{n}} = \lim_{n\to\infty}\frac{5}{1+\frac{\sqrt{n^2-5n}}{n}} \xleftarrow{\text{rename to}} \sqrt{n^2}$$

$$= \lim_{n\to\infty}\frac{5}{1+\sqrt{\frac{n^2-5n}{n^2}}} = \lim_{n\to\infty}\frac{5}{1+\sqrt{1-\frac{5}{n}}} \xleftarrow{\to 0 \text{ as } n\to\infty}$$

$$= \frac{5}{1+\sqrt{1}} = \boxed{\frac{5}{2}} \neq 0 \quad \boxed{\begin{array}{l}\text{The series diverges}\\\text{by the Test for divergence}\end{array}}$$

II. Alternating Series Test

$$b_n = \ln\left(1+\frac{2}{n^2}\right) \qquad \xleftarrow{\to 0 \text{ as } n\to\infty} \text{ and } \ln 1 = 0$$

① $\displaystyle\lim_{n\to\infty} b_n = \lim_{n\to\infty}\ln\left(1+\frac{2}{n^2}\right) = 0$

② $b_{n+1} < b_n \qquad \ln\left(1+\frac{2}{(n+1)^2}\right) < \ln\left(1+\frac{2}{n^2}\right)$

$\underbrace{\qquad\qquad}_{\text{smaller}}$

$\boxed{\text{The series converges by the Alternating Series Test}}$

4.2 Determine whether the series converges or diverges.

I. $\displaystyle\sum_{n=1}^{\infty}\left(\ln\left(\sqrt{e}+\frac{1}{n}\right)\right)^{n+1}$

II. $\displaystyle\sum_{n=1}^{\infty}\frac{n^{\sqrt{3}}}{e^{n+4}5^{n}}$

4.2 Determine whether the series converges or diverges.

I. $\displaystyle\sum_{n=1}^{\infty}\left(\ln\left(\sqrt{e}+\frac{1}{n}\right)\right)^{n+1}$

II. $\displaystyle\sum_{n=1}^{\infty}\frac{n^{\sqrt{3}}}{e^{n+4}\,5^{n}}$

I. Root Test

$$\lim_{n\to\infty}\left(|a_n|\right)^{\frac{1}{n}}=\lim_{n\to\infty}\left[\ln\left(\sqrt{e}+\frac{1}{n}\right)^{n+1}\right]^{\frac{1}{n}}=\lim_{n\to\infty}\ln\left(\sqrt{e}+\frac{1}{n}\right)^{1+\frac{1}{n}}$$

$\frac{1}{n}\to 0$ as $n\to\infty$ $\qquad = \ln\left(\sqrt{e}+0\right)^{1}=\frac{1}{2}\ln e=\frac{1}{2}<1$

The series converges by the Root Test

II. Ratio Test

$$\lim_{n\to\infty}\left|\frac{a_{n+1}}{a_n}\right|=\lim_{n\to\infty}\left|\frac{(n+1)^{\sqrt{3}}}{n^{\sqrt{3}}}\cdot\frac{e^{n+4}}{e^{n+5}}\cdot\frac{5^{n}}{5^{n+1}}\right|$$

$$=\lim_{n\to\infty}\left|1\cdot\frac{e^{n+4}}{e^{n+4}\cdot e}\cdot\frac{5^{n}}{5^{n}\cdot5}\right|=\frac{1}{5e}<1$$

since
deg·num=deg·den.

The series converges by the Ratio Test

4.3 Determine whether the series converges or diverges.

I. $\displaystyle\sum_{n=1}^{\infty} \frac{1}{n\left(1+\left(\ln n\right)^2\right)}$

II. $\displaystyle\sum_{n=1}^{\infty} \frac{1}{2\sqrt[3]{n} - \sqrt[5]{n}}$

4.3 Determine whether the series converges or diverges.

I. $\displaystyle\sum_{n=1}^{\infty} \frac{1}{n\left(1+(\ln n)^2\right)}$

II. $\displaystyle\sum_{n=1}^{\infty} \frac{1}{2\sqrt[3]{n}-\sqrt[5]{n}}$

I. Integral Test

$f(x) = \dfrac{1}{x\left(1+(\ln x)^2\right)}$

$f(x)$ is
(A) positive
(b) Continuous
(c) decreasing

Consider
$\displaystyle\int_{1}^{\infty} f(x)\,dx$

$\displaystyle\int_{1}^{\infty} \frac{1}{x\left(1+(\ln x)^2\right)}\,dx$

$u = \ln x$
$du = \frac{1}{x}dx$

$\displaystyle\int_{0}^{\infty} \frac{1}{1+u^2}\,du = \arctan u$

$x=1 \Rightarrow u=0$
$x\to\infty \Rightarrow u\to\infty$

$= \displaystyle\lim_{b\to\infty} \arctan u \Big|_0^b$

$= \underbrace{\displaystyle\lim_{b\to\infty} \arctan b}_{\pi/2} - \underbrace{\arctan 0}_{0} = \frac{\pi}{2} \Rightarrow$ The integral converges

> The series converges by the Integral Test

II. Direct Comparison Test

$b_n = \dfrac{1}{2\sqrt[3]{n}}$ $\displaystyle\sum_{n=1}^{\infty} b_n = \frac{1}{2}\sum_{n=1}^{\infty} \frac{1}{n^{1/3}}$ Divergent p-series $p = 1/3 < 1$

$a_n = \dfrac{1}{2\sqrt[3]{n}-\sqrt[5]{n}}$ has a smaller denom (all other parts are the same)

a_n is larger

$b_n < a_n$ so $\sum a_n$ will also diverge

> The series diverges by the Direct Comparison Test

4.4 Determine whether the series converges or diverges.

I. $\displaystyle\sum_{n=1}^{\infty}\left(\frac{n+3}{2n-5}\right)^{n}$

II. $\displaystyle\sum_{n=1}^{\infty}\sqrt[4]{\frac{2}{n^3}}$

4.4 Determine whether the series converges or diverges.

I. $\displaystyle\sum_{n=1}^{\infty}\left(\frac{n+3}{2n-5}\right)^{n}$

II. $\displaystyle\sum_{n=1}^{\infty}\sqrt[4]{\frac{2}{n^{3}}}$

I. Root Test

$$\lim_{n\to\infty}\left(|a_n|\right)^{\frac{1}{n}} = \lim_{n\to\infty}\left[\left(\frac{n+3}{2n-3}\right)^{n}\right]^{\frac{1}{n}} = \lim_{n\to\infty}\frac{n+3}{2n-3} = \frac{1}{2} < 1$$

The series converges by the Root Test

II. P-series

$$\sum_{n=1}^{\infty}\sqrt[4]{\frac{2}{n^3}} = \sum_{n=1}^{\infty}\left(\frac{2}{n^3}\right)^{1/4} = 2^{1/4}\underbrace{\sum_{n=1}^{\infty}\frac{1}{n^{3/4}}}_{\substack{Dw. \ p\text{-series} \\ p=\frac{3}{4}<1}}$$

The series is a divergent p-series

4.5 Determine whether the series converges or diverges.

I. $\displaystyle\sum_{n=1}^{\infty}\frac{n^2}{\left(n^3+1\right)^3}$

II. $\displaystyle\sum_{n=1}^{\infty}\frac{2+\sin(n)}{\sqrt{n^5}}$

4.5 Determine whether the series converges or diverges.

I. $\displaystyle\sum_{n=1}^{\infty} \frac{n^2}{\left(n^3+1\right)^3}$ II. $\displaystyle\sum_{n=1}^{\infty} \frac{2+\sin(n)}{\sqrt{n^5}}$

I. Direct Comparison Test

$b_n = \dfrac{n^2}{n^9} = \dfrac{1}{n^7}$ $\displaystyle\sum_{n=1}^{\infty} \frac{1}{n^7}$ is a convergent p-series
$p = 7 > 1$

$a_n = \dfrac{n^2}{(n^3+1)^3}$ has a larger denom. than b_n
all other parts $=$, so we have

$a_n < b_n$ a larger denom makes a smaller fraction

> The series converges by the Direct Comp. Test

II. Direct Comparison

$-1 \le \sin n \le 1$

$1 \le 2+\sin n \le 3$

$\dfrac{1}{n^{5/2}} \le \underbrace{\dfrac{2+\sin n}{n^{5/2}}} \le \dfrac{3}{n^{5/2}}$

$b_n = \dfrac{3}{n^{5/2}}$ $\displaystyle\sum_{n=1}^{\infty} \frac{3}{n^{5/2}}$ is a convergent p-series

$a_n \le b_n$

> The series converges by the Direct Comp. Test

4.6 Determine whether the series converges or diverges.

I. $\displaystyle\sum_{n=2}^{\infty} \frac{\ln n}{\sqrt{n^3}}$

II. $\displaystyle\sum_{n=1}^{\infty} \frac{\sqrt{n+4}}{n^2}$

4.6 Determine whether the series converges or diverges.

I. $\displaystyle\sum_{n=2}^{\infty} \frac{\ln n}{\sqrt{n^3}}$ II. $\displaystyle\sum_{n=1}^{\infty} \frac{\sqrt{n+4}}{n^2}$

I. Integral Test

$f(x) = \dfrac{\ln x}{x^{3/2}}$ $f(x)$ is $\begin{cases} \text{positive} \\ \text{continuous} \\ \text{decreasing} \end{cases}$ Consider $\displaystyle\int_{2}^{\infty} f(x)\,dx$

$\displaystyle\int_{2}^{\infty} \frac{\ln x}{x^{3/2}}\,dx$ Integration by parts

$u = \ln x$ $dv = x^{-3/2}$

$du = \frac{1}{x}\,dx$ $v = x^{-1/2} \cdot -2$

$= \lim_{b\to\infty}\left[\dfrac{-\ln x - 8}{2\sqrt{x}}\right]_{2}^{b}$

$uv - \int v\,du$

$= \lim_{b\to\infty} \dfrac{-\ln b - 8}{2\sqrt{b}} + \dfrac{\ln 2 + 8}{2\sqrt{2}}$ $= \dfrac{-\ln x}{2\sqrt{x}} + \int 2x^{-3/2}\,dx$

$\stackrel{\infty}{=}\stackrel{\infty}{=}$ use L'Hôpital's Rule $= \dfrac{-\ln x}{2\sqrt{x}} - \dfrac{4}{\sqrt{x}} = \dfrac{-\ln x - 8}{2\sqrt{x}}$

$= \lim_{b\to\infty} \dfrac{-\frac{1}{b}}{\frac{1}{\sqrt{b}}} = \lim_{b\to\infty} \dfrac{-1}{b}\sqrt{b} = \lim_{n\to\infty} \dfrac{-1}{\sqrt{b}} = 0$

The integral converges to $\dfrac{\ln 2 + 8}{2\sqrt{2}}$

The series also converges by the Integral Test

II. Limit Comparison Test

$b_n = \dfrac{\sqrt{n}}{n^2} = \dfrac{1}{n^{3/2}}$ $\displaystyle\sum b_n = \sum_{n=1}^{\infty} \frac{1}{n^{3/2}}$ convergent p-series $(p = 3/2 < 1)$

$\displaystyle\lim_{n\to\infty} \frac{a_n}{b_n} = \lim_{n\to\infty} \frac{\frac{\sqrt{n+4}}{n^2}}{\frac{1}{n^{3/2}}} = \lim_{n\to\infty} \frac{\sqrt{n+4}}{n^2}\cdot n^{3/2}$ $\uparrow \sqrt{n^3}$

$= \displaystyle\lim_{n\to\infty} \frac{\sqrt{(n+4)\cdot n^3}}{n^2} = \lim_{n\to\infty} \frac{\sqrt{n^4 + 4n^3}}{n^2} = 1$ so they behave alike

The series converges by the Limit Comp. Test

4.7 Determine whether the series converges or diverges.

I. $\displaystyle\sum_{n=1}^{\infty} \frac{n! \cdot (n-1)! \cdot 5^n}{(2n+1)!}$

II. $\displaystyle\sum_{n=1}^{\infty} \left(\cos\left(\frac{1}{n}\right)\right)^{n^2}$

4.7 Determine whether the series converges or diverges.

I. $\displaystyle\sum_{n=1}^{\infty} \frac{n!\cdot(n-1)!\cdot 5^n}{(2n+1)!}$

II. $\displaystyle\sum_{n=1}^{\infty}\left(\cos\left(\frac{1}{n}\right)\right)^{n^2}$

I. Ratio Test

$$\lim_{n\to\infty}\left|\frac{a_{n+1}}{a_n}\right| = \lim_{n\to\infty}\left|\frac{(n+1)!\cdot n!}{n!\cdot(n-1)!}\cdot\frac{5^{n+1}}{5^n}\cdot\frac{(2n+1)!}{(2n+3)!}\right|$$

$$=\lim_{n\to\infty}\left|\frac{(n+1)\,n!}{n!}\cdot\frac{n\cdot(n-1)!}{(n-1)!}\cdot\frac{5^n\cdot 5}{5^n}\cdot\frac{(2n+1)!}{(2n+3)(2n+2)(2n+1)!}\right|$$

$$=\lim_{n\to\infty}\frac{(n+1)\cdot n\cdot 5}{(2n+3)(2n+2)}=\lim_{n\to\infty}\frac{5n^2+5n}{4n^2+10n+6}=\frac{5}{4}>1$$

> The series diverges by the Ratio Test

II. Test for Divergence

$$\lim_{n\to\infty}\left(\cos\left(\tfrac{1}{n}\right)\right)^{n^2}="1^{\infty}"\leftarrow\text{indeterminant power}$$

$$y=\lim_{n\to\infty}\left(\cos\left(\tfrac{1}{n}\right)\right)^{n^2}\quad\text{take } \ln$$

$$\ln y=\lim_{n\to\infty}\ln\left(\cos\left(\tfrac{1}{n}\right)\right)^{n^2}=\lim_{n\to\infty}n^2\ln\left(\cos\left(\tfrac{1}{n}\right)\right)="\infty\cdot 0"$$

$$\ln y=\lim_{n\to\infty}\frac{\ln\left(\cos\left(\tfrac{1}{n}\right)\right)}{\tfrac{1}{n^2}}="\frac{0}{0}"\quad\text{use L'Hôpital's Rule}$$

$$\ln y\overset{L'H}{=}\lim_{n\to\infty}\frac{\frac{1}{\cos(1/n)}\cdot-\sin\left(\tfrac{1}{n}\right)\cdot\tfrac{-1}{n^2}}{\tfrac{-2}{n^3}}=\lim_{n\to\infty}\frac{-\tan\left(\tfrac{1}{n}\right)\cdot\tfrac{-1}{n^2}\cdot\underbrace{\tfrac{n^3}{-2}}_{\tfrac{n}{2}}}{}$$

$$\ln y=\lim_{n\to\infty}\frac{-\tan\left(\tfrac{1}{n}\right)}{\tfrac{2}{n}}="\frac{0}{0}"\overset{L'H}{=}\lim_{n\to\infty}\frac{-\sec^2\left(\tfrac{1}{n}\right)\cdot\tfrac{-1}{n^2}}{\tfrac{-2}{n^2}}$$

$$\ln y=\lim_{n\to\infty}\frac{-\sec^2\left(\tfrac{1}{n}\right)}{2}=\frac{-1}{2}\qquad e^{\ln y}=e^{\frac{-1}{2}}\quad y=e^{-1/2}=\frac{1}{\sqrt{e}}\neq 0$$

> The series diverges by the Test for Divergence

4.8. Determine whether the following series is absolutely convergent, conditionally convergent or divergent.

I. $\displaystyle\sum_{n=2}^{\infty} \frac{(-1)^n \ln n}{n^{3/4}}$

II. $\displaystyle\sum_{n=1}^{\infty} \frac{(n+2)!}{e^{n^2}}$

4.8. Determine whether the following series is absolutely convergent, conditionally convergent or divergent.

I. $\displaystyle\sum_{n=2}^{\infty} \frac{(-1)^n \ln n}{n^{3/4}}$

II. $\displaystyle\sum_{n=1}^{\infty} \frac{(n+2)!}{e^{n^2}}$

I. $\displaystyle\sum_{n=2}^{\infty} |a_n| = \sum_{n=2}^{\infty} \frac{\ln n}{n^{3/4}}$ $\underline{\text{Diverges}}$ by the Direct Comp. Test

with $b_n = \frac{1}{n^{3/4}}$ $\sum b_n$ is a divergent p-series

$b_n < a_n$ since $1 < \ln n$ for $n \geq 3$

$\displaystyle\sum_{n=2}^{\infty} \frac{(-1)^n \ln n}{n^{3/4}}$ converges by the Alternating Series Test

$b_n = \frac{\ln n}{n^{3/4}}$ ① $\displaystyle\lim_{n \to \infty} \frac{\ln n}{n^{3/4}} = 0$ $n^{3/4}$ grows faster

② $\frac{\ln(n+1)}{(n+1)^{3/4}} < \frac{\ln n}{n^{3/4}}$ den. grow faster than num.

$\boxed{\text{The series is conditionally convergent}}$

II. The series isn't alternating so it is either absolutely convergent or divergent.

Use Ratio Test

$\displaystyle\lim_{n \to \infty} \left| \frac{a_{n+1}}{a_n} \right| = \lim_{n \to \infty} \left| \frac{(n+3)!}{(n+2)!} \cdot \frac{e^{n^2}}{e^{(n+1)^2}} \right|$ $(n+1)^2 = n^2 + 2n + 1$

$= \displaystyle\lim_{n \to \infty} \left| \frac{(n+3)(n+2)!}{(n+2)!} \cdot \frac{e^{n^2}}{e^{n^2} \cdot e^{2n+1}} \right|$

$= \displaystyle\lim_{n \to \infty} \frac{n+3}{e^{2n+1}} = 0 < 1$ e^{2n+1} grows faster than $n+3$

$\boxed{\text{The series is absolutely convergent}}$

182

4.9. Determine whether the following series is absolutely convergent, conditionally convergent or divergent.

I. $\displaystyle\sum_{n=1}^{\infty} \frac{(-1)^n}{n + \ln n}$

II. $\displaystyle\sum_{n=1}^{\infty} \frac{(-1)^{n-1} (n!)^3}{(3n)!}$

4.9. Determine whether the following series is absolutely convergent, conditionally convergent or divergent.

I. $\displaystyle\sum_{n=1}^{\infty} \frac{(-1)^n}{n + \ln n}$

II. $\displaystyle\sum_{n=1}^{\infty} \frac{(-1)^{n-1}(n!)^3}{(3n)!}$

I. $\displaystyle\sum_{n=1}^{\infty} |a_n| = \sum_{n=1}^{\infty} \frac{1}{n+\ln n}$ Use Limit Comp. test

$$b_n = \frac{1}{n} \quad \sum \frac{1}{n} \text{ div. Harmonic}$$

$$\lim_{n\to\infty} \frac{a_n}{b_n} = \lim_{n\to\infty} \frac{\frac{1}{n+\ln n}}{\frac{1}{n}} = \lim_{n\to\infty} \frac{n}{n+\ln n} = 1$$

$\ln n$ negligible when $n\to\infty$

So they behave alike and $\sum|a_n|$ diverges.

$$\sum_{n=1}^{\infty} \frac{(-1)^n}{n+\ln n} \quad \text{use Alternating Series Test}$$

$$b_n = \frac{1}{n+\ln n} \quad \textcircled{1} \lim_{n\to\infty} \frac{1}{n+\ln n} = 0$$
$$\textcircled{2}\ b_{n+1} < b_n$$
$\Big\}$ the series converges by the AST

The series is conditionally convergent

II. $\displaystyle\sum |a_n| = \sum_{n=1}^{\infty} \frac{n! \cdot n! \cdot n!}{(3n)!}$ use Ratio Test

$$\lim_{n\to\infty}\left|\frac{a_{n+1}}{a_n}\right| = \lim_{n\to\infty}\left| \frac{(n+1)!}{n!} \cdot \frac{(n+1)!}{n!} \cdot \frac{(n+1)!}{n!} \cdot \frac{(3n)!}{(3n+3)!}\right|$$

$$= \lim_{n\to\infty}\left| \frac{(n+1)\cdot n!}{n!} \cdot \frac{(n+1)\cdot n!}{n!} \cdot \frac{(n+1)\cdot n!}{n!} \cdot \frac{(3n)!}{(3n+3)(3n+2)(3n+1)(3n)!}\right|$$

$$= \lim_{n\to\infty} \frac{(n+1)^3}{(3n+3)(3n+2)(3n+1)} = \frac{1}{27} < 1$$

deg num = deg den.

The series converges absolutely

184

4.10. Determine whether the following series is absolutely convergent, conditionally convergent or divergent.

I. $\displaystyle\sum_{n=1}^{\infty} \frac{(-e)^n}{(2.71)^n}$ II. $\displaystyle\sum_{n=1}^{\infty} \frac{1}{\sqrt{n}\left(\sqrt{n}+1\right)^3}$

4.10. Determine whether the following series is absolutely convergent, conditionally convergent or divergent.

I. $\displaystyle\sum_{n=1}^{\infty} \frac{(-e)^n}{(2.71)^n}$

II. $\displaystyle\sum_{n=1}^{\infty} \frac{1}{\sqrt{n}\left(\sqrt{n}+1\right)^3}$

I. $\sum |a_n| = \displaystyle\sum_{n=1}^{\infty}\left(\frac{e}{2.71}\right)^n$ Geometric Series

with $r = \frac{e}{2.71} > 1$

$e \approx 2.7182$

$e > 2.71$

Diverges

$\sum a_n$ will also diverge   now $r = \frac{-e}{2.71}$

$|r| > 1$

$\boxed{\text{The series diverges}}$

II. The series is not alternating so it either
Converges absolutely or diverges.

Direct compare to $b_n = \frac{1}{\sqrt{n} \cdot \sqrt{n}^3} = \frac{1}{n^2}$

$\sum \frac{1}{n^2}$ converges p-series $p > 1$

$a_n < b_n$

$\underbrace{\frac{1}{\sqrt{n}(\sqrt{n}+1)^3}}_{\substack{\text{larger den.}\\\text{so smaller}}} < \frac{1}{\sqrt{n}(\sqrt{n})^3}$

$\boxed{\text{The series is absolutely convergent}}$

186

4.11. Determine whether the following series is absolutely convergent, conditionally convergent or divergent.

I. $\displaystyle\sum_{n=1}^{\infty} \frac{(-1)^{n+1}}{n\sqrt{n+2}}$

II. $\displaystyle\sum_{n=2}^{\infty} \frac{(-1)^{n}\, n^{2/3}}{\ln n}$

4.11. Determine whether the following series is absolutely convergent, conditionally convergent or divergent.

I. $\displaystyle\sum_{n=1}^{\infty} \frac{(-1)^{n+1}}{n\sqrt{n+2}}$
II. $\displaystyle\sum_{n=2}^{\infty} \frac{(-1)^n\, n^{2/3}}{\ln n}$

I. $\displaystyle\sum_{n=1}^{\infty} |a_n| = \sum_{n=1}^{\infty} \frac{1}{n\sqrt{n+2}}$ Direct compare to $b_n = \frac{1}{n\sqrt{n}}$

$\sum \frac{1}{n\sqrt{n}}$ conv. p-series $p = \frac{3}{2} > 1$

$\begin{array}{c} a_n < b_n \\ \dfrac{1}{n\sqrt{n+2}} < \dfrac{1}{n\sqrt{n}} \end{array}$ larger denom $\rightarrow$ smaller fraction all other parts same

> The series is absolutely convergent

II. $\displaystyle\sum |a_n| = \sum_{n=2}^{\infty} \frac{n^{3/2}}{\ln n}$ $\displaystyle\lim_{n\to\infty} \frac{n^{3/2}}{\ln n} = \infty$

Diverges by the Test for DIV. $n^{3/2}$ grows faster than $\ln n$

$\sum a_n$ will still diverge $\displaystyle\lim_{n\to\infty} \frac{(-1)^n \cdot n^{3/2}}{\ln n}$ DNE

$\begin{cases} \infty & n \text{ is even} \\ -\infty & n \text{ is odd} \end{cases}$

> The series diverges

188

4.12. Find the interval of convergence of the power series.

$$\sum_{n=1}^{\infty} \frac{(n+1)(2x+1)^n}{2^n n^2}$$

(A) $\left(\frac{-3}{2}, \frac{1}{2}\right]$ (E) $\left(1, 2\right]$

(B) $\left[\frac{-3}{2}, \frac{1}{2}\right]$ (F) $\left[1, 2\right]$

(C) $\left(\frac{-3}{2}, \frac{1}{2}\right)$ (G) $\left\{\frac{-1}{2}\right\}$

(D) $\left[\frac{-3}{2}, \frac{1}{2}\right)$ (H) $\left(-\infty, \infty\right)$

4.12. Find the interval of convergence of the power series.

$$\sum_{n=1}^{\infty} \frac{(n+1)(2x+1)^n}{2^n n^2}$$

(A) $\left(\frac{-3}{2}, \frac{1}{2}\right]$ (E) $\left(1, 2\right]$

(B) $\left[\frac{-3}{2}, \frac{1}{2}\right]$ (F) $\left[1, 2\right]$

(C) $\left(\frac{-3}{2}, \frac{1}{2}\right)$ (G) $\left\{\frac{-1}{2}\right\}$

(D) $\left[\frac{-3}{2}, \frac{1}{2}\right)$ (H) $\left(-\infty, \infty\right)$

$$\lim_{n \to \infty} \left| \frac{a_{n+1}}{a_n} \right| = \lim_{n \to \infty} \left| \frac{n+2}{n+1} \cdot \frac{(2x+1)^{n+1}}{(2x+1)^n} \cdot \frac{2^n}{2^{n+1}} \cdot \frac{n^2}{(n+1)^2} \right|$$

$$= \lim_{n \to \infty} \left| 1 \cdot \frac{(2x+1) \cdot (2x+1)}{(2x+1)} \cdot \frac{2^n}{2^n \cdot 2} \cdot 1 \right|$$

$$\left| \frac{2x+1}{2} \right| \quad \overset{force}{<} 1$$

$$\Rightarrow |2x+1| < 2$$

$-2 < 2x+1 < 2$
$-1 \quad -1 \quad -1$

$\dfrac{-3}{2} < \dfrac{2x}{2} < \dfrac{1}{2}$

$\dfrac{-3}{2} < x < \dfrac{1}{2}$

$\underline{X = \frac{-3}{2}}$

$$\sum_{n=1}^{\infty} \frac{(n+1)(-2)^n}{2^n \cdot n^2} = \sum_{n=1}^{\infty} \frac{(-1)^n \cdot (n+1)}{n^2}$$

$\boxed{\text{Conv.}}$ by AST

$b_n = \frac{n+1}{n^2} = \frac{1}{n} + \frac{1}{n^2}$

$\lim_{n \to \infty} b_n = 0 / b_n$ is decr.

$\underline{x = \frac{1}{2}}$

$$\sum_{n=1}^{\infty} \frac{(n+1)2^n}{n^2 \cdot 2^n}$$

$$\sum_{n=1}^{\infty} \frac{n+1}{n^2} = \sum_{n=1}^{\infty} \frac{1}{n} + \frac{1}{n^2}$$

$$\underbrace{\sum_{n=1}^{\infty} \frac{1}{n}}_{DIV} + \underbrace{\sum_{n=1}^{\infty} \frac{1}{n^2}}_{CONV.} \quad \boxed{DIV}$$

$$\boxed{\left[\frac{-3}{2}, \frac{1}{2}\right)}$$

4.13. Find the interval of convergence of the power series.

$$\sum_{n=1}^{\infty} \frac{(-1)^n (2x-3)^n}{2n+1}$$

(A) $(-1,2]$ (E) $(1,2]$
(B) $(-1,2)$ (F) $[1,2]$
(C) $(1,2)$ (G) $[-1,2]$
(D) $[1,2)$ (H) $(-\infty,\infty)$

4.13. Find the interval of convergence of the power series.

$$\sum_{n=1}^{\infty} \frac{(-1)^n (2x-3)^n}{2n+1}$$

(A) $(-1,2]$ (E) $(1,2]$

(B) $(-1,2)$ (F) $[1,2]$

(C) $(1,2)$ (G) $[-1,2]$

(D) $[1,2)$ (H) $(-\infty,\infty)$

$$\lim_{n\to\infty}\left|\frac{a_{n+1}}{a_n}\right| = \lim_{n\to\infty}\left|\frac{(-1)^{n+1}}{(-1)^n}\cdot\frac{(2x-3)^{n+1}}{(2x-3)^n}\cdot\frac{2n+1}{2n+3}\right|$$

$$= \lim_{n\to\infty}\left|\frac{(-1)^n(-1)}{(-1)^n}\cdot\frac{(2x-3)^n(2x-3)}{(2x-3)^n}\cdot\frac{2n+1}{2n+3}\right|$$

force

$$|-1\cdot(2x-3)| < 1$$

$$|-1|\cdot|2x-3| < 1$$
     1

$x = 1$

$$\sum_{n=1}^{\infty}\frac{(-1)^n\cdot(-1)^n}{2n+1} = \sum_{n=1}^{\infty}\frac{1}{2n+1}$$

LCT with $b_n = \frac{1}{2n}$

$\sum\frac{1}{2n}$ div. (Harmonic)

$$\lim_{n\to\infty}\frac{a_n}{b_n} = \frac{\frac{1}{2n+1}}{\frac{1}{2n}} = 1$$

So they behave alike

$$\boxed{Div.}$$

$$-1 < 2x-3 < 1$$
$$+3 \qquad +3 \quad +3$$
$$\frac{2}{2} < \frac{2x}{2} < \frac{4}{2}$$
$$1 < x < 2$$

$x = 2$

$$\sum_{n=1}^{\infty}\frac{(-1)^n}{2n+1} \quad \boxed{Conv} \text{ by AST}$$
$$\text{with } b_n = \frac{1}{2n+1}$$

1) $\lim_{n\to\infty} b_n = 0$

2) b_n is decreasing

$$\boxed{(-1,2]}$$

4.14. Find the interval of convergence of the power series.

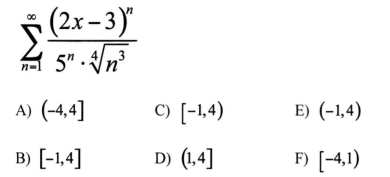

$$\sum_{n=1}^{\infty} \frac{(2x-3)^n}{5^n \cdot \sqrt[4]{n^3}}$$

A) $(-4,4]$ C) $[-1,4)$ E) $(-1,4)$

B) $[-1,4]$ D) $(1,4]$ F) $[-4,1)$

4.14. Find the interval of convergence of the power series.

$$\sum_{n=1}^{\infty} \frac{(2x-3)^n}{5^n \cdot \sqrt[4]{n^3}}$$

A) $(-4,4]$ C) $[-1,4)$ E) $(-1,4)$

B) $[-1,4]$ D) $(1,4]$ F) $[-4,1)$

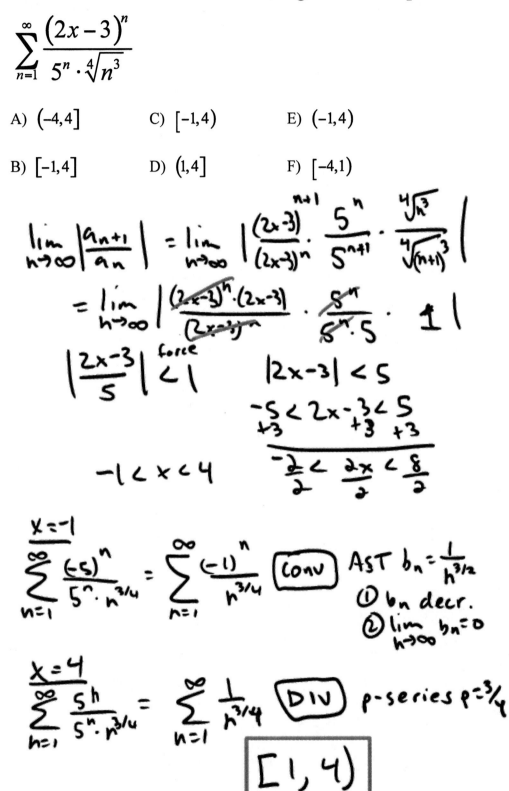

$$\lim_{n\to\infty} \left| \frac{a_{n+1}}{a_n} \right| = \lim_{n\to\infty} \left| \frac{(2x-3)^{n+1}}{(2x-3)^n} \cdot \frac{5^n}{5^{n+1}} \cdot \frac{\sqrt[4]{n^3}}{\sqrt[4]{(n+1)^3}} \right|$$

$$= \lim_{n\to\infty} \left| \frac{(2x-3)^n \cdot (2x-3)}{(2x-3)^n} \cdot \frac{5^n}{5^n \cdot 5} \cdot 1 \right|$$

$$\left| \frac{2x-3}{5} \right| \overset{force}{<} 1 \qquad |2x-3| < 5$$

$$-5 < 2x-3 < 5$$
$$+3 \qquad +3 \quad +3$$
$$\frac{-2}{2} < \frac{2x}{2} < \frac{8}{2}$$

$$-1 < x < 4$$

$\underline{x=-1}$

$$\sum_{n=1}^{\infty} \frac{(-5)^n}{5^n \cdot n^{3/4}} = \sum_{n=1}^{\infty} \frac{(-1)^n}{n^{3/4}} \quad \boxed{Conv} \quad AST \ b_n = \frac{1}{n^{3/4}}$$

① b_n decr.
② $\lim_{n\to\infty} b_n = 0$

$\underline{x=4}$

$$\sum_{n=1}^{\infty} \frac{5^n}{5^n \cdot n^{3/4}} = \sum_{n=1}^{\infty} \frac{1}{n^{3/4}} \quad \boxed{DIV} \quad p\text{-series } p = 3/4$$

$$\boxed{[1,4)}$$

4.15. Find the coefficient on x^6 in the Maclaurin series for $f(x) = \cosh(2x)$ using the identity $\cosh(x) = \dfrac{1}{2}\left(e^x + e^{-x}\right)$

(A) 1

(B) $\dfrac{4}{45}$

(C) $\dfrac{2}{3}$

(D) 2

(E) $\dfrac{1}{24}$

(F) $\dfrac{1}{720}$

(G) $\dfrac{8}{35}$

(H) $\dfrac{2}{315}$

4.15. Find the coefficient on x^6 in the Maclaurin series for $f(x) = \cosh(2x)$ using the identity $\cosh(x) = \frac{1}{2}\left(e^x + e^{-x}\right)$

(A) 1

(B) $\dfrac{4}{45}$

(C) $\dfrac{2}{3}$

(D) 2

(E) $\dfrac{1}{24}$

(F) $\dfrac{1}{720}$

(G) $\dfrac{8}{35}$

(H) $\dfrac{2}{315}$

$$e^x = 1 + x + \frac{x^2}{2!} + \frac{x^3}{3!} + \frac{x^4}{4!} + \frac{x^5}{5!} + \frac{x^6}{6!} + \cdots$$

$$+ \quad e^{-x} = 1 - x + \frac{x^2}{2!} - \frac{x^3}{3!} + \frac{x^4}{4!} - \frac{x^5}{5!} + \frac{x^6}{6!}$$

$$\rule{8cm}{0.4pt}$$

$$e^x + e^{-x} = 2 + 2\left(\frac{x^2}{2!}\right) + 2\left(\frac{x^4}{4!}\right) + 2\left(\frac{x^6}{6!}\right) + \cdots$$

$$\frac{e^x + e^{-x}}{2} = 1 + \frac{x^2}{2!} + \frac{x^4}{4!} + \frac{x^6}{6!} + \cdots = \cosh(x)$$

$$\cosh(2x) = 1 + \frac{(2x)^2}{2!} + \frac{(2x)^4}{4!} + \frac{(2x)^6}{6!} + \cdots$$

$$\text{Coeff on } x^6 = \frac{2^6}{6!} = \frac{64}{720} = \frac{8}{90} = \boxed{\frac{4}{45}}$$

4.16. Find the third degree Taylor polynomial for $f(x) = x^{3/2}$ centered at $x = 4$.

4.16. Find the third degree Taylor polynomial for $f(x) = x^{3/2}$ centered at $x = 4$.

$$f(x) = x^{3/2} \qquad f(4) = 4^{3/2} = 8 \div 0! = 8$$

$$f'(x) = \frac{3}{2}x^{1/2} \qquad f'(4) = \frac{3}{2}\sqrt{4} = 3 \div 1! = 3(x-4)$$

$$f''(x) = \frac{3}{4} \cdot x^{-1/2} \qquad f''(4) = \frac{3}{4} \cdot \frac{1}{\sqrt{4}} = \frac{3}{8} \div 2! = \frac{3}{16}(x-4)^2$$

$$f'''(x) = -\frac{3}{8}x^{-3/2} \qquad f'''(4) = \frac{-3}{8} \cdot \frac{1}{4^{3/2}} = \frac{-3}{64} \div 3! = \frac{-3}{64 \cdot 6} = \frac{-1}{128}(x-4)^3$$

$$\boxed{T_3(x) = \frac{-1}{128}(x-4)^3 + \frac{3}{16}(x-4)^2 + 3(x-4) + 8}$$

4.17. Evaluate the limit

$$\lim_{x \to 0} \frac{x^2 + x\ln(1-x)}{xe^{-5x} - x + 5x^2}.$$

(A) 1

(B) $\dfrac{1}{4}$

(C) $\dfrac{-1}{100}$

(D) $\dfrac{-1}{15}$

(E) $\dfrac{-1}{10}$

(F) $\dfrac{-1}{5}$

(G) $\dfrac{-1}{50}$

(H) $\dfrac{-1}{25}$

4.17. Evaluate the limit

$$\lim_{x\to 0}\frac{x^2 + x\ln(1-x)}{xe^{-5x} - x + 5x^2}.$$

(A) 1   (E) $\dfrac{-1}{10}$

(B) $\dfrac{1}{4}$ (F) $\dfrac{-1}{5}$

(C) $\dfrac{-1}{100}$ (G) $\dfrac{-1}{50}$

(D) $\dfrac{-1}{15}$ (H) $\dfrac{-1}{25}$

$$\ln(1-x) = -x - \frac{x^2}{2} - \frac{x^3}{3} - \cdots$$

$$e^x = 1 + x + \frac{x^2}{2!} + \frac{x^3}{3!} + \cdots$$

$$e^{-5x} = 1 - 5x + \frac{25x^2}{2} - \frac{125x^3}{6} + \cdots$$

$$\lim_{x\to 0}\frac{x^2 + x\left(-x - \frac{x^2}{2} - \frac{x^3}{3}\right)}{x\left(1 - 5x + \frac{25x^2}{2} - \frac{125x^3}{6} + \cdots\right) - x + 5x^2}$$

$$= \lim_{x\to 0}\frac{x^2 - x^2 - \frac{x^3}{2} - \frac{x^4}{3} \cdots}{\left(x - 5x^2 + \frac{25}{2}x^3 + \cdots\right) - x + 5x^2}$$

$$= \lim_{x\to 0}\frac{-\frac{x^3}{2} - \frac{x^4}{3} - \cdots}{\frac{25}{2}x^3 - \frac{125}{6}x^4 + \cdots} \cdot \frac{\frac{1}{x^3}}{\frac{1}{x^3}}$$

$$= \lim_{x\to 0}\frac{-\frac{1}{2} - \frac{1}{3}x + \text{higher order terms}}{\frac{25}{2} - \frac{125}{6}x + \text{higher order terms}} \xrightarrow{\text{as } x\to 0}$$

$$= \frac{\frac{-1}{2}}{\frac{25}{2}} = \frac{-1}{2}\cdot\frac{2}{25} = \boxed{\frac{-1}{25}}$$

200

4.18. Evaluate the limit

$$\lim_{x \to 0} \frac{1 - \cos(2x)}{x(e^{3x} - 1)}$$

(A) 0   (E) $\dfrac{1}{3}$

(B) ∞ (F) $\dfrac{2}{3}$

(C) 1   (G) $\dfrac{1}{2}$

(D) 2   (H) $\dfrac{1}{4}$

4.18. Evaluate the limit

$$\lim_{x \to 0} \frac{1 - \cos(2x)}{x\left(e^{3x} - 1\right)}$$

(A) 0

(B) ∞

(C) 1

(D) 2

(E) $\frac{1}{3}$

(F) $\frac{2}{3}$

(G) $\frac{1}{2}$

(H) $\frac{1}{4}$

$$\cos x = 1 - \frac{x^2}{2!} + \frac{x^4}{4!} + \cdots$$

$$\cos 2x = 1 - \frac{(2x)^2}{2} + \frac{(2x)^4}{24} + \cdots$$

$$e^x = 1 + x + \frac{x^2}{2} + \frac{x^3}{6} + \cdots$$

$$e^{3x} = 1 + 3x + \frac{9x^2}{2} + \frac{27x^3}{6} + \cdots$$

$$= \lim_{x \to 0} \frac{1 - \left(1 - 2x^2 + \frac{16}{24}x^4 + \cdots\right)}{x\left[\left(1 + 3x + \frac{9}{2}x^2 + \cdots\right) - 1\right]}$$

$$= \lim_{x \to 0} \frac{\left(2x^2 - \frac{2}{3}x^4 + \cdots\right)\frac{1}{x^2}}{\left(3x^2 + 9x^3 + \cdots\right)\frac{1}{x^2}}$$

$$= \lim_{x \to 0} \frac{2 - \frac{2}{3}x^2 + \text{higher order terms} \longrightarrow 0 \text{ as } x \to 0}{3 + 9x + \text{''} \quad \text{''} \longrightarrow 0 \text{ as } x \to 0} = \boxed{\frac{2}{3}}$$

202

4.19. If $f(x) = x^3 \cos(x^2)$, find $f^{(11)}(0)$, the value of the eleventh derivative evaluated at 0.

(A) 1

(B) $\dfrac{1}{24}$

(C) $\dfrac{121}{16}$

(D) $\dfrac{13}{6}$

(E) $\dfrac{-10!}{5!}$

(F) $\dfrac{11!}{4!}$

(G) $\dfrac{11}{5}$

(H) $\dfrac{11}{4}$

4.19. If $f(x) = x^3 \cos(x^2)$, find $f^{(11)}(0)$, the value of the eleventh derivative evaluated at 0.

(A) 1

(B) $\dfrac{1}{24}$

(C) $\dfrac{121}{16}$

(D) $\dfrac{13}{6}$

(E) $\dfrac{-10!}{5!}$

(F) $\dfrac{11!}{4!}$

(G) $\dfrac{11}{5}$

(H) $\dfrac{11}{4}$

$$\cos x = 1 - \frac{x^2}{2!} + \frac{x^4}{4!} - \frac{x^6}{6!} + \cdots$$

$$\cos(x^2) = 1 - \frac{(x^2)^2}{2!} + \frac{(x^2)^4}{4!} - \frac{(x^2)^6}{6!} + \cdots$$

$$\cos(x^2) = 1 - \frac{x^4}{2!} + \frac{x^8}{4!} - \frac{x^{12}}{6!} + \cdots$$

$$x^3 \cdot \cos(x^2) = x^3 - \frac{x^7}{2!} + \frac{x^{11}}{4!} - \frac{x^{15}}{6!} + \cdots$$

$$\boxed{\text{Coeff. on } x^{11} = \frac{1}{4!}}$$

Maclaurin series in general:

$$f(0) + f'(0)x + \frac{f''(0)}{2!}x^2 + \frac{f'''(0)}{3!}x^3 + \cdots + \frac{f^{(11)}(0)}{11!}x^{11} + \cdots$$

$$\boxed{\text{Coeff. on } x^{11} = \frac{f^{(11)}(0)}{11!}}$$

They must equal: $\dfrac{1}{4!} = \dfrac{f^{(11)}(0)}{11!}$

$$\Rightarrow \boxed{f^{(11)}(0) = \frac{11!}{4!}}$$

204

4.20. Find the third degree Taylor polynomial for $f(x) = \sqrt[3]{x}$ centered at $x = 1$.

4.20. Find the third degree Taylor polynomial for $f(x) = \sqrt[3]{x}$ centered at $x = 1$.

$f(x) = x^{1/3}$

$f(1) = 1 \div 0! = 1$

$f'(x) = \frac{1}{3}x^{-2/3}$

$f'(1) = \frac{1}{3} \div 1! = \frac{1}{3}(x-1)$

$f''(x) = \frac{-2}{9}x^{-5/3}$

$f''(1) = \frac{-2}{9} \div 2! = \frac{-1}{9}(x-1)^2$

$f'''(x) = \frac{-2}{9} \cdot \frac{-5}{3} \cdot x^{-8/3}$

$f'''(1) = \frac{10}{27} \div 3! = \frac{\overset{5}{\cancel{10}}}{27 \cdot \underset{3}{\cancel{6}}} = \frac{5}{81}(x-1)^3$

$$T_3(x) = \frac{5}{81}(x-1)^3 - \frac{1}{9}(x-1)^2 + \frac{1}{3}(x-1) + 1$$

4.21. Evaluate the limit

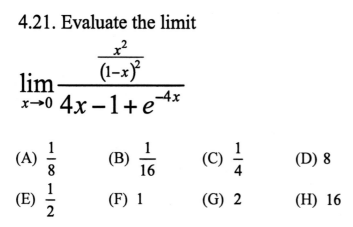

$$\lim_{x \to 0} \frac{\dfrac{x^2}{(1-x)^2}}{4x - 1 + e^{-4x}}$$

(A) $\dfrac{1}{8}$ (B) $\dfrac{1}{16}$ (C) $\dfrac{1}{4}$ (D) 8

(E) $\dfrac{1}{2}$ (F) 1   (G) 2   (H) 16

4.21. Evaluate the limit

$$\lim_{x \to 0} \frac{\dfrac{x^2}{(1-x)^2}}{4x - 1 + e^{-4x}}$$

(A) $\dfrac{1}{8}$ (B) $\dfrac{1}{16}$ (C) $\dfrac{1}{4}$ (D) 8

(E) $\dfrac{1}{2}$ (F) 1   (G) 2   (H) 16

$$\frac{1}{(1-x)^2} = 1 + 2x + 3x^2 + 4x^3 + \cdots$$

$$\frac{x^2}{(1-x)^2} = x^2 + 2x^3 + 3x^4 + 4x^5$$

$$e^x = 1 + x + \frac{x^2}{2!} + \frac{x^7}{7!} + \cdots$$

$$e^{-4x} = 1 - 4x + \frac{(-4x)^2}{2} + \frac{(4x)^3}{3!} + \cdots$$

$$\lim_{x \to 0} \frac{x^2 + 2x^3 + 3x^4 + 4x^5}{4x - 1 + \left(1 - 4x + 8x^2 - \frac{64x^3}{6} + \cdots\right)}$$

$$= \lim_{x \to 0} \frac{\left(x^2 + 2x^3 + 3x^4 + 4x^5 + \cdots\right)\frac{1}{x^2}}{\left(8x^2 - \frac{32}{3}x^3 + \cdots\right)\frac{1}{x^2}}$$

$$= \lim_{x \to 0} \frac{1 + 2x + 3x^2 + 4x^3 + \cdots \to 0}{8 - \frac{32}{3}x + \cdots \to 0} = \boxed{\frac{1}{8}}$$

4.22. Find the coefficient on x^4 in the Maclaurin series for
$$f(x) = xe^{-2x}$$

(A) $\dfrac{2}{3}$ (B) $\dfrac{4}{3}$ (C) $\dfrac{-8}{3}$ (D) $-\dfrac{2}{3}$

(E) $-\dfrac{4}{3}$ (F) -2 (G) 2 (H) -1

4.22. Find the coefficient on x^4 in the Maclaurin series for

$$f(x) = xe^{-2x}$$

(A) $\dfrac{2}{3}$ (B) $\dfrac{4}{3}$ (C) $\dfrac{-8}{3}$ (D) $-\dfrac{2}{3}$

(E) $-\dfrac{4}{3}$ (F) -2 (G) 2 (H) -1

$$e^x = 1 + x + \frac{x^2}{2!} + \frac{x^3}{3!} + \frac{x^4}{4!}$$

$$e^{-2x} = 1 - 2x + \frac{(-2x)^2}{2!} + \frac{(-2x)^3}{3!} + \frac{(-2x)^4}{4!} + \cdots$$

$$xe^{-2x} = x - 2x^2 + \frac{4x^3}{2} - \frac{8x^4}{6} + \cdots$$

$$\text{Coeff. on } x^4 = \boxed{\dfrac{-4}{3}}$$

4.23. Find the sum of the series

$$\ln\left(1+2+\frac{2^2}{2!}+\frac{2^3}{3!}+\cdots\right)+\left(1+\frac{2}{3}+\frac{4}{9}+\frac{8}{27}+\cdots\right)$$

(A) 5   (B) 4   (C) 3   (D) 2   (E) 1   (F) diverges

4.23. Find the sum of the series

$$\ln\left(1+2+\frac{2^2}{2!}+\frac{2^3}{3!}+\cdots\right)+\left(1+\frac{2}{3}+\frac{4}{9}+\frac{8}{27}+\cdots\right)$$

(A) 5   (B) 4   (C) 3   (D) 2   (E) 1   (F) diverges

$$\ln\left(1+2+\frac{2^2}{2!}+\frac{2^3}{3!}+\cdots\right)+\left(1+\frac{2}{3}+\frac{4}{9}+\frac{8}{27}+\cdots\right)$$

e^x power series w/ x replaced by 2

Geometric w/ $r=\frac{2}{3}$ first term 1

$$\ln(e^2) + \frac{1}{1-\frac{2}{3}}$$

$$2 + \frac{1}{\frac{1}{3}} = 2+3 = \boxed{5}$$

212

4.24. Evaluate the limit

$$\lim_{x \to 0} \frac{\arctan x - x \cos x - \frac{1}{6} x^3}{x^5}$$

(A) $\dfrac{53}{150}$ (C) $\dfrac{7}{3}$ (E) $\dfrac{14}{3}$ (G) $\dfrac{46}{15}$

(B) $\dfrac{31}{5}$ (D) $\dfrac{52}{5}$ (F) $\dfrac{62}{5}$ (H) $\dfrac{19}{120}$

4.24. Evaluate the limit

$$\lim_{x \to 0} \frac{\arctan x - x\cos x - \frac{1}{6}x^3}{x^5}$$

(A) $\dfrac{53}{150}$ (C) $\dfrac{7}{3}$ (E) $\dfrac{14}{3}$ (G) $\dfrac{46}{15}$

(B) $\dfrac{31}{5}$ (D) $\dfrac{52}{5}$ (F) $\dfrac{62}{5}$ (H) $\dfrac{19}{120}$

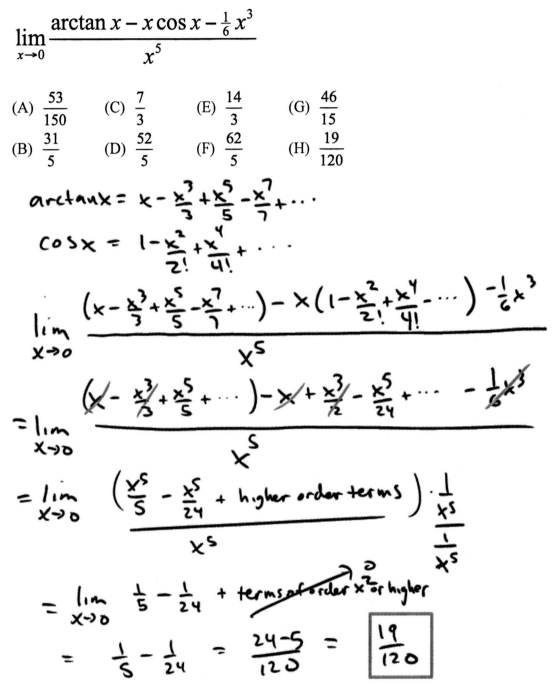

$$\arctan x = x - \frac{x^3}{3} + \frac{x^5}{5} - \frac{x^7}{7} + \cdots$$

$$\cos x = 1 - \frac{x^2}{2!} + \frac{x^4}{4!} + \cdots$$

$$\lim_{x \to 0} \frac{\left(x - \frac{x^3}{3} + \frac{x^5}{5} - \frac{x^7}{7} + \cdots\right) - x\left(1 - \frac{x^2}{2!} + \frac{x^4}{4!} - \cdots\right) - \frac{1}{6}x^3}{x^5}$$

$$= \lim_{x \to 0} \frac{\left(x - \frac{x^3}{3} + \frac{x^5}{5} + \cdots\right) - x + \frac{x^3}{2} - \frac{x^5}{24} + \cdots - \frac{1}{6}x^3}{x^5}$$

$$= \lim_{x \to 0} \frac{\left(\frac{x^5}{5} - \frac{x^5}{24} + \text{higher order terms}\right) \cdot \frac{1}{x^5}}{x^5 \cdot \frac{1}{x^5}}$$

$$= \lim_{x \to 0} \frac{1}{5} - \frac{1}{24} + \text{terms of order } x^2 \text{ or higher}$$

$$= \frac{1}{5} - \frac{1}{24} = \frac{24-5}{120} = \boxed{\frac{19}{120}}$$

4.25. Find the second order Taylor polynomial for $f(x) = x^{2/3}$ centered at $x = 8$.

4.25. Find the second order Taylor polynomial for $f(x) = x^{2/3}$ centered at $x = 8$.

$f(x) = x^{2/3}$ $f(8) = 8^{2/3} = 2^2 = 4 \div 0! = 4$

$f'(x) = \frac{2}{3}x^{-1/3}$ $f'(8) = \frac{2}{3 \cdot 8^{1/3}} = \frac{1}{3} \div 1! = \frac{1}{3}$

$f''(x) = \frac{-2}{9}x^{-4/3}$ $f''(8) = \frac{-2}{9 \cdot 8^{4/3}} = \frac{-2}{9 \cdot 16} = \frac{-1}{72} \div 2! = \frac{-1}{144}$

$$T_2(x) = \frac{-1}{144}(x-8)^2 + \frac{1}{3}(x-8) + 4$$

INDEX

CPSIA information can be obtained
at www.ICGtesting.com
Printed in the USA
LVOW09s1243150118
562979LV00046B/2934/P